CHINESE PICTOGRAMS

**TYPE DESIGN / VISUAL IDENTITY /
POSTER / BOOK DESIGN**

*The Pictographic Evolution
& Graphic Creation of Hanzi*

SP
SendPoints

CHINESE PICTOGRAMS

The Pictographic Evolution
& Graphic Creation of Hanzi

© 2019 SendPoints Publishing Co., Ltd.

EDITED & PUBLISHED BY SendPoints Publishing Co., Ltd.

PUBLISHER: Lin Gengli

PUBLISHING DIRECTOR: Lin Shijian

ASSISTANT PUBLISHING-DIRECTOR: Chen Ting

CHIEF EDITOR: Lin Shijian

LEAD EDITOR: Kit Leung

EXECUTIVE EDITOR: Stephanie He

DESIGN DIRECTOR: Lin Shijian

EXECUTIVE ART EDITOR: Kit Leung

PROOFREADING: James N. Powell, Stephanie He, Li Weiji

REGISTERED ADDRESS: Room 15A Block 9 Tsui Chuk Garden, Wong Tai Sin, Kowloon, Hong Kong

TEL: +852-35832323 / **FAX:** +852-35832448

OFFICE ADDRESS: 7F, 9th Anning Street, Jinshazhou, Baiyun District, Guangzhou, China

TEL: +86-20-89095121 / **FAX:** +86-20-89095206

BEIJING OFFICE: Room 107, Floor 1, Xiyingfang Alley, Ande Road, Dongcheng District, Beijing, China

TEL: +86-10-84139071 / **FAX:** +86-10-84139071

SHANGHAI OFFICE: Room 307, Building 1, Hong Qiang Creative, Zhabei District, Shanghai, China

TEL: +86-21-63523469 / **FAX:** +86-21-63523469

SALES MANAGER: Kris Guo

TEL: +86-20-81007895

EMAIL: sales@sendpoints.cn

WEBSITE: www.sendpoints.cn / www.spbooks.cn

ISBN 978-988-79284-9-2

Preface

Chinese characters or Hanzi, the only official language of China. This ideographic writing system has had a profound influence on the history of language. Hanzi was once commonly used in Japan, Korean Peninsula, etc. Nowadays, some Hanzi are still retained as a part of Japanese writing systems.

Based on the methods of character formation and usage, Chinese characters fall into six different categories: pictograms, simple ideograms, compound ideograms, phono-semantic compounds, transformed cognates and phonetic loan characters. The earliest form of Chinese writing is the oracle bone script, originally drawings of natural objects. This script—carved on turtle shells and animal bones—was used by officials in ancient times for conducting divinations. Thus, the name "oracle bones" was used to describe these animal bones as well as the Oracle Bone script of writing symbols that was etched on them.

The etchings derived from the pictorial images are called pictograms. The only pictographic language in use today is the Dongba symbols of the Naxi people and the Sui script of the Sui people. However, the pictographic writing system has its inevitable limitation—certain physical objects and abstract concepts simply cannot be depicted by graphic symbols. Yet this interesting writing system has played a significant role in the development of Chinese characters.

The vast number of Chinese characters can be intimidating, yet the commonly used Chinese characters are only 5,000 to 6,000, among which only 3,000 characters are needed for basic literacy. In the several thousands of years of Chinese writing evolution, the writing of Chinese characters has changed over time and appeared in a wide variety of styles. The Oracle Bone Script, Bronze Script, Seal Script, Clerical Script, Cursive Script, Regular Script, and Cursive Script are known as the seven major writing styles of the language. Nowadays, a simplified Chinese script is used in mainland China, whereas the traditional Chinese script is still used in Hong Kong, Macau, and Taiwan.

In the creative sphere, the manifestations and applications of Chinese characters varied in multiple aspects. In the field of graphic design, Hanzi as an important element of visual communication has had a significant influence on the creation of visual expression. Designers tend to decompose and recreate Chinese characters based on their glyph so as to bring strong visual impact. (In type design, a character is an abstract concept with semantic value as a sign or symbol in written language, while a glyph is a particular visual representation of a character.) This book revolves around Chinese characters, divided into three parts—the invention and development of Chinese character, the glyphic evolution of Hanzi, and projects based on hanzi. The first part illustrates the development and impact of Chinese character through its invention, its evolution of calligraphy, and its influence on neighboring cultures. The second part presents a selection of 132 characters with their evolution from Oracle Bone Script, Bronze Script, Seal Script, Cursive Script, Semi-cursive Script, Imitation Song, Song, to Gothic, and from Traditional Chinese to Simplified Chinese. The third part features outstanding graphic design projects worldwide based on the use of Chinese characters. This book seeks to provide readers with fresh perspectives to explore the history and value of Chinese characters.

By Lin Shijian,
SendPoints Publishing co., Ltd.

The *Invention*
& Development
of Hanzi

Rubbings of scripts on Xiaochenyu
Rhinoceros-shaped Ritual Vessel
(The script describes the Emperor of
the Shang Dynasty conquering the foreign states)

© Mountain, Wikipedia

San Family Plate, with 357 characters in bronze
script, in the Western Zhou Dynasty(1046BC—
771BC), the earliest land contract in China

© Janson 22, Wikipedia

The Invention of Chinese Characters

Chinese characters or Hanzi, the writing system of the Chinese language, is the world's oldest living writing system. This means that unlike the scripts of ancient Egypt, Babylon, and India, Chinese characters are the only writing system originating in ancient times that has been passed down to the present. Thus, some scholars have listed Chinese characters as the fifth great invention of China.

The origins of Chinese characters are mysterious. According to legends, it was Cangjie, the official historian under the Yellow Emperor, who invented Chinese characters. As political affairs became increasingly demanding, a shared set of symbols for communicating was needed. Cangjie was ordered to collect and sort out various tribal scripts. His study of the footprints of birds and beasts, the landscapes of the earth, and the stars in the sky is believed to have been a great source of inspiration in his invention of Chinese characters.

Archaeological discoveries have seen a great number of symbols engraved on pottery and jades of the late Neolithic period. Some of the symbols share many similarities with the primitive Chinese characters. It is believed that these pictographs later evolved to become signs for communication. In the early 2nd century Chinese character dictionary *Shuowen Jiezi*, the author Xu Shen (c.58-c.148) gave definitions for the already well-known six principles of character formation and usage, known as *Liushu*, based on which Chinese characters fall into six different categories: pictograms, simple ideograms, compound ideograms, phono-semantic compounds, transformed cognates and phonetic loan characters. Transformed cognates and phonetic loan characters were developed using the forms or pronunciations of the existing characters in the first four categories. Thus, this chapter is confined to the four main types of Chinese character: pictograms, simple ideograms, compound ideograms, and phono-semantic compounds.

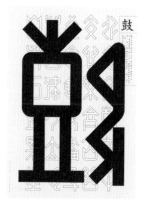

Modern Artistic Recreation of Oracle Bone Script

© Tang Shipeng

A Portrayal of the Yellow Emperor

© Gan Bozong,
Wikimedia Commons

A Portrayal of Cangjie, the mythical
inventor of the Chinese writing system

© Li Ung Bing,
Wikimedia Commons

Pictograms

Characters in this class were created by sketching, via the lines or strokes, the objects they denote. For example, the character "馬" (horse) resembles a real horse with mane and four legs, and the character "魚" (fish) resembles a real fish with its head, body, and tail. Due to their inability to denote abstract concepts, only a small portion of Chinese characters were created by this method. Once the symbolic nature of pictograms was developed, some Chinese characters in this class were used to denote abstract concepts rather than concrete objects. For instance, the character "大" (big) resembles the shape of a person standing upright with arms and legs spread. Using this method, adjectives derived from nouns emerged, though this method was difficult to be applied widely.

The oracle bone script of "horse" (馬), "fish" (魚), and "big" (大).
© *Erin Silversmith, Micheletb, Wikimedia Commons*

Simple Ideograms

Simple ideograms show the abstract thinking in the invention of Chinese characters, a result of the people's ability to see the universality and extract the essence of things around them. Simple ideograms can be divided into two categories: simple ideograms, that only consist of ideographic symbols, such as "上" (up), "下" (down); simple ideograms that combines pictograms and ideographic signs, for instance, "刃" (knife edge), where a dot was placed on the character "刀" (knife) to indicate the sharp part of a knife. As to the second category, there has been disputes about the border between pictograms and simple ideograms. A now generally accepted definition of simple ideograms is: any sign without an obvious image in real life or phonetic indicator.

oracle bone script—
"Sky" (天)

oracle bone script—
"Knife Edge" (刃)

oracle bone script—
"Up" (上)

oracle bone script—
"Down" (下)

Compound Ideograms

Compound ideograms are also known as "logical aggregates", because characters in this class are combinations of two or more pictographic or ideographic characters. Together they indicate a new meaning. For example, the character "酒" (liquor) results from the combination of the signs "氵" (water) and "酉" (earthen jar to contain liquor). The character "解" is another example. It combines the signs "角" (horn), "刀" (knife), and "牛" (cattle), meaning "to dissect".

knife   cattle   horn   to dissect

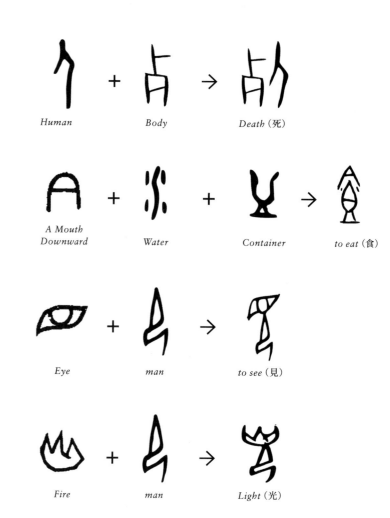

Human	Body	Death（死）	

A Mouth Downward	Water	Container	to eat（食）

Eye	man	to see（見）

Fire	man	Light（光）

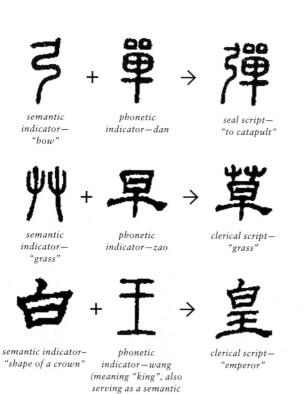

semantic indicator— "bow" + *phonetic indicator—dan* → *seal script— "to catapult"*

semantic indicator— "grass" + *phonetic indicator—zao* → *clerical script— "grass"*

semantic indicator– "shape of a crown" + *phonetic indicator—wang (meaning "king", also serving as a semantic indicator)* → *clerical script— "emperor"*

Phono-semantic Compounds

In spite of the invention of compound ideograms, there were meanings that could not be expressed by placing three or more pictographic or ideographic characters together. To remedy this situation, the ancient Chinese invented phono-semantic compounds, which make up the largest category of characters. These characters consist of two parts: a semantic indicator (often graphically simplified) and a phonetic indicator. The semantic indicator suggests the general meaning of the character, whereas the phonetic indicator indicates the pronunciation: via a phonological similarity to another character. For example, the character "弹" (pronounced dan and meaning "to catapult") is composed of its semantic indicator "弓" (bow), and its phonetic indicator "單" (pronounced dan). And the character "草" (pronounced cao and meaning "grass") is another example. It is composed of its semantic indicator "艹" and its phonetic indicator "早" (pronounced zao). Phono-semantic compounds are invented based on pictograms, simple ideograms, and compound ideograms, but they successfully connect symbols with pronunciation, which is a great leap from ideograms to phonograms.

Inscription for Liquan Spring of Jiucheng Palace
by Ouyang Xun (557—641),
a Chinese calligrapher of the Tang dynasty

© *Wikimedia Commons*

The Evolution of Chinese Characters

In the course of over 6000 years, Chinese characters have undergone many changes, from which there are seven distinctive styles developed in different periods of time: the Oracle Bone Script, the Bronze Script, the Seal Script, the Clerical Script, the Regular Script, the Cursive Script, and the Semi-cursive Script. Visually, Chinese characters had become straight line-based and highly stylized, with its pictorial quality weakening constantly. Regardless of the changes, the square ideographic script remains highly recognizable and informative as a graphic symbol itself. Moreover, its calligraphy boasts diverse styles and unique aesthetic appeal.

According to historical records, there have been two interrelated types of changes: natural and revolutionary. Natural changes have taken place in the language due to the effects of temporal and geographical distance. In different eras and locales, the rising number of characters evolved multiple pronunciations and meanings. This always leads to a lack of consistency and standardization. Thus, after a certain period of divergent evolution due to the natural flow of time and the flow of the language into different geographical regions, revolutionary changes have been needed to ensure communication. Revolutionary changes arise to complement and counteract the excesses of natural changes, and to satisfy the development of productivity as society progresses. These revolutionary changes arise from the conscious and active regulation as well as standardization of the use of Chinese characters. These changes have normally been discontinuous, intense, and completed within a short period of time.

Rubbing of Three Scripts Stone Classics inscribed in 241,
renowned for its inscriptions of the Ancient Script,
the Small Seal Script, and the Clerical Script, for each character

© *San Lie, WikimediaCommons*

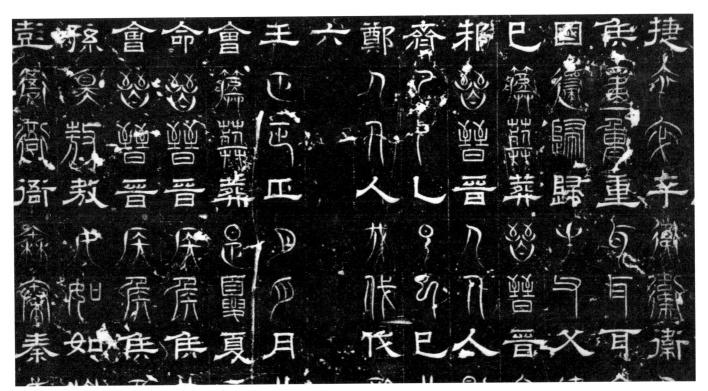

The evolution of character
象 *(elephant)*

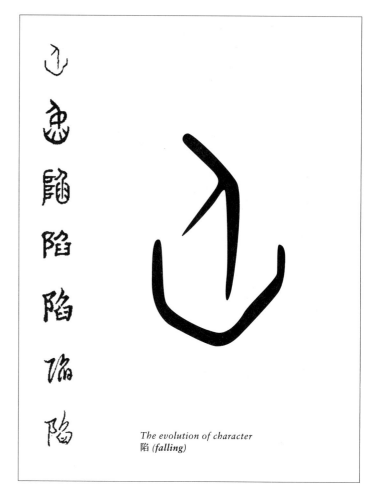

The evolution of character
陷 *(falling)*

Inscribed Symbols

There is an old Chinese saying: calligraphy and painting share the same origin. It was because the earliest Chinese scripts were derived from symbols and drawings, which gradually evolved into ideograms. Those inscribed symbols reflect the nature of primitive scripts and are recognized as one of the sources of Chinese characters. The inscribed symbols were discovered in Jiahu (6500 BC), Shuangdun (5000 BC), Banpo (4000 BC), Qingdun (3000 BC), etc.

Neolithic signs in
Jiahu archaeological site, China

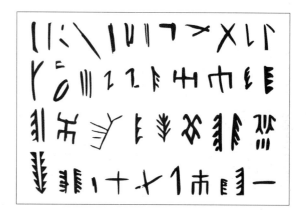

Neolithic signs in
Banpo archaeological site, China

Piece of a Chinese oracle bone,
from Henan (Anyang), Shang Dynasty, 1200 BC.
Now in the Musée de Mariemont, Belgium

© *BabelStone, Wikimedia Commons*

Oracle bone from the reign of King Wu Ding
(late Shang dynasty c.1200–1050 BC).

© *Vassil, Wikimedia Commons*

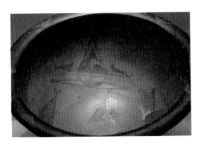

Basin with a fish pattern
with a human face

© *Zhangzhugang,*
Wikimedia Commons

Basin with a fish pattern

© *Zhangzhugang,*
Wikimedia Commons

Oracle Bone Script

The Oracle Bone Script is the earliest discovered ancient Chinese script, a relatively complete writing system dating back to the late Shang dynasty (1600BC—1046BC). Most oracle bone inscriptions are records of divinations on tortoises shells or animal bones. After the demise of the Shang and Zhou dynasties, the Oracle Bone Script was used for a period of time. Judging from the identifiable 1,500 oracle characters, scholars argue that the character-composing methods of pictograms, simple ideograms, compound ideograms, and phono-semantic compounds had already been invented.

Tortoise plastron with
divination inscription from
the Shang dynasty,
dating to the reign of King Wu Ding

© *BabelStone, Wikimedia Commons*

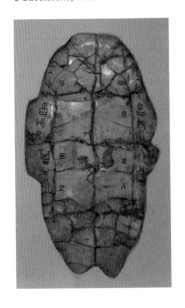

→
Some oracle bones from
the Shang Dynasty,
now preserved in the
Linden-Museum in Germany

© *Dr. Meierhofer(left),*
Herr Klugbeisser(right),
Wikimedia Commons

Lid of Zewang Gui from the mid Western Zhou Dynasty with bronze inscription inside

© *Ghost Bunny, Wikipedia*

Bronze Inscriptions

There was another script in use in the Shang dynasty in addition to the oracle inscription: bronze inscriptions. They had been used for more than 1,200 years, from the Shang dynasty to the end of the Spring and Autumn Period (770BC–221BC). This script is called the Bronze Script was because the characters were cast in bronze bells and vessels–symbols of power and status. Based on the identifiable 2,420 characters, included in *Jinwen Bian*, the most basic reference work of bronze inscriptions, most of them are compound ideograms, vivid as drawings. And the content of those bronze in-scriptions concerns the achievements of ancestors and princes as well as records of major historical events.

The couplet written in large seal script by Zhang Taiyan (1868–1936), a Chinese philologist, textual critic, philosopher, and revolutionary in the late Qing Dynasty

© *Wikimedia Commons*

Large Seal Script

Originating from the late Western Zhou dynasty (1046 BC –771 BC), the Large Seal Script was widely used in the State of Qin during the Spring and Autumn Period (770 BC–221 BC). The Large Seal Script is roughly referred to scripts before the emergence of the Small Seal Script, so it is transitional. It shows two significant developments: the lines became straighter, simpler, and more even, and the structure was in better order, laying the foundation of the block feature of Chinese characters.

An old rubbing of seal script inscriptions on drum-shaped stone blocks from the Eastern Zhou Dynasty

© *Wikimedia Commons*

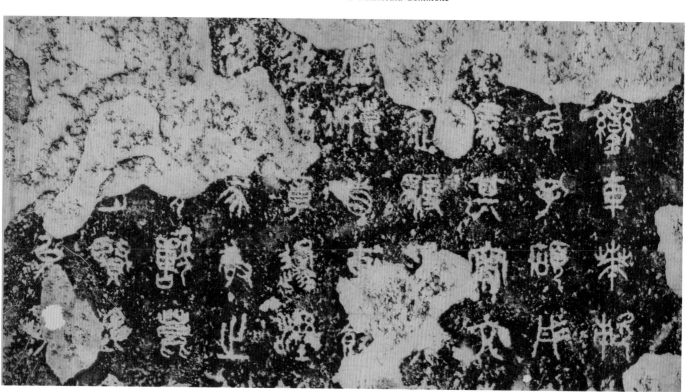

Small Seal Script

Basing on the Large Seal Script, the Prime Minister of the Qin dynasty (221BC—207BC) unified variant forms of characters in different states, transforming them into the Small Seal Script as the formal script for China. Compared to the Large Seal Script, the Small Seal Script is more concise, regular, and coordinated, with more orderly character patterns and weaker pictorial features. More importantly, this reform rendered all characters as rough block shapes. The Small Seal Script was popularly used until the late Western Han dynasty(202BC—AD8), when it was replaced by the Clerical Script.

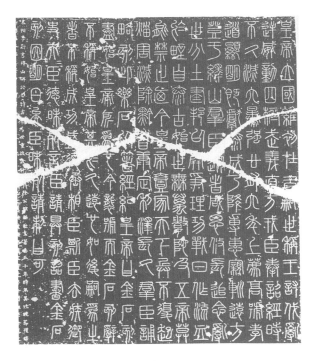

A replica of Yishan Keshi
by Zheng Wenbao in the Song dynasty (993),
written in the Small Seal Script

© *Wikimedia Commons*

A replica of Yishan Keshi
by Zheng Wenbao in the Song
dynasty (993),
written in the Small Seal Script

© *Wikimedia Commons*

Clerical Script

The Clerical Script assumed its immature, "proto-clerical" form in the State of Qin during the Warring States period. It was more concise than the Small Seal Script, but assumed a kind of vulgar and less- standardized form, which nevertheless became popular. When the Emperor Qin Shi Huang standardized the writing system, the writing of the Clerical Script was influenced as well. To achieve a more convenient and effective way of writing, the Clerical Script was developed into a broader and flatter shape, with its horizontal strokes longer than the vertical ones. The emergence of the Clerical Script marked a milestone in the history of Chinese characters, for it marks a watershed between pictorial scripts and straight-line based scripts, which are composed of horizontal strokes, vertical strokes, left-falling strokes, dots, turning strokes, etc. Furthermore, several modifications and simplifications made in the clerical script set the basic form for present-day characters.

Xiping Stone Classics inscribed
from 175–183 during
the Eastern Han Dynasty

© *Ayelie, Wikimedia Commons*

Regular Script

The Regular Script first appeared in the Eastern Han dynasty (25–220), as a script evolved from, yet more simplified and upright than the Clerical Script. With the addition of the pause technique, the strokes such as "hook" and "turning" were created, and new strokes such as "long falling" and "short falling" were introduced to the Regular Script, making its structure more complete. The new script was called the Regular Script because of its neatness, and developed into the dominant modern Chinese script.

Imperial Order Presented to Yue Fei
written by Emperor Gaozong (r. 1127–1162),
in the Regular Script, with elements of the Semi-Cursive Script

© *Wikimedia Commons*

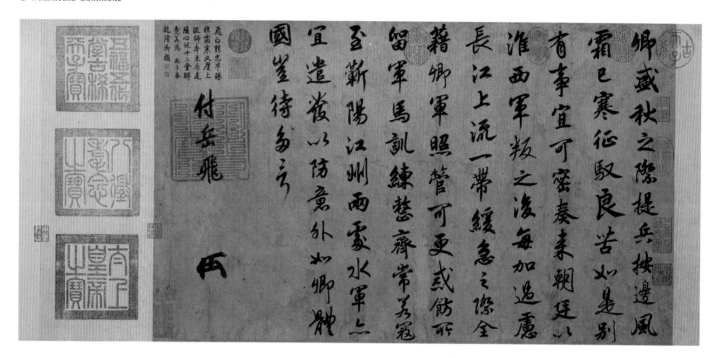

Cursive Script

Formed in the Han dynasty (202 BC–220), the Cursive Script evolved from the Clerical Script, and has three categories: Clerical Cursive, Modern Cursive, and Wild Cursive. As its name suggests, Clerical Cursive was initially derived from the Clerical Script, and with its maturation, the Cursive Script began to evolve its own rules and orders, while retaining its flexibility. The three characteristics of the Cursive Script are its simple structure; its use of dots or strokes to replace certain parts of characters; and its unbroken strokes, which make writing faster and emotion expression possible.

Timely Clearing After Snowfall,
written in modern cursive script by
Wang Hsi-chih (303–361)
from Chin dynasty, generally regarded as
the greatest Chinese calligrapher in history

© *Wikimedia Commons*

Semi-cursive Script

The Semi-Cursive Script was developed on the basis of the Regular Script, and made its appearance in the late Eastern Han dynasty. In fact, it is a script between Regular Script and Cursive Script, to remedy the slow writing of the Regular Script and the difficulty of reading the Cursive Script. Thus, the Semi-Cursive Script is more legible than the Cursive Script but not as neat as the Regular Script, and so with higher practicability and artistry.

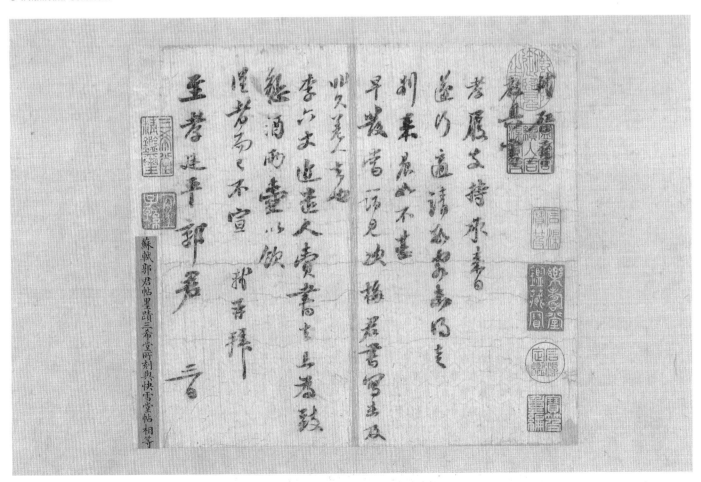

趣舍萬殊靜躁不同當其欣
於所遇暫得於己快然自足不
知老之將至及其所之既惓情
隨事遷感慨係之矣向之所
欣俛仰之間以為陳迹猶不
能不以之興懷況修短隨化終
期於盡古人云死生亦大矣豈
不痛哉每攬昔人興感之由
若合一契未嘗不臨文嗟悼不
能喻之於懷固知一死生為虛
誕齊彭殤為妄作後之視今
亦由今之視昔悲夫故列
敘時人錄其所述雖世殊事
異所以興懷其致一也後之攬
者亦將有感於斯文

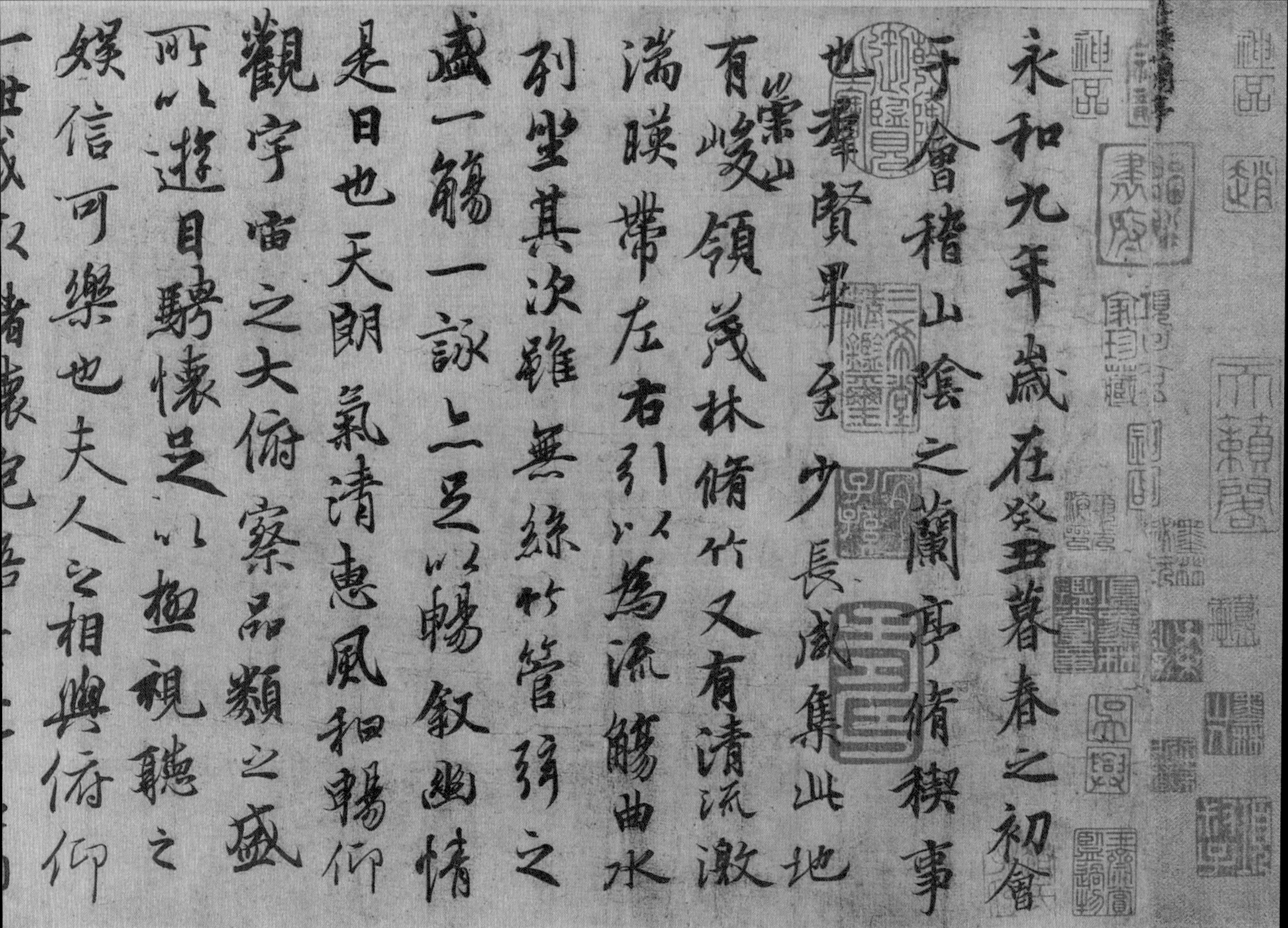

永和九年歲在癸丑暮春之初會
于會稽山陰之蘭亭修禊事
也羣賢畢至少長咸集此地
有崇山峻領茂林修竹又有清流激
湍暎帶左右引以為流觴曲水
列坐其次雖無絲竹管弦之
盛一觴一詠亦足以暢敘幽情
是日也天朗氣清惠風和暢仰
觀宇宙之大俯察品類之盛
所以遊目騁懷足以極視聽之
娛信可樂也夫人之相與俯仰

*Main text of a Tang dynasty copy of Wang Xizhi's **Lantingji Xu** by Feng Chengsu in Semi-cursive Script*

Simplified Chinese Characters

Night shot of HongKong,
traditional Chinese characters used in signboards

© Allen

Chinese characters have evolved during their long history. In a broad sense, simplified Chinese characters are those characters that assumed vulgar forms and variants in history. In a narrower sense, simplified Chinese characters refer to those prescribed in documents such as *List of the First Group of Standardized Forms of Variant Characters* (1955), *Chinese Character Simplification Scheme* (1956), *Complete List of Simplified Characters* (1964 and 1986), and *List of Generally Used Characters in Modern Chinese* (1988) issued by the People's Republic of China and used in mainland China with the purpose of encouraging literacy. Some rules were applied to simplify the characters. Some are composed of the simplified graphic or phonetic indicators stylized from popular cursive or semi-cursive forms. Others were modifications of variants and characters in popular forms. Some were created by the rules composing compound ideograms and phono-semantic compounds, etc. Presently, simplified Chinese characters are widely used in mainland China, whereas traditional characters are still in use in Hong Kong, Macau, and Taiwan.

Comparison of characters in
***Chinese Character Simplification Draft** (1955)*
*and **Chinese Character Simplification Scheme** (1956)*

© Stomatapoll, Wikimedia Commons

Traditional	幹	虜	麼	頸	艦	獎	牽	顯
Draft	仐	虏	庅	頚	艦	奖	牵	顕
Simplified	干	虏	么	颈	舰	奖	牵	显
Traditional	鑿	燦	憂	嚴	臨	癰	膚	導
Draft	凿	粲	夏	严	临	痈	肩	孕
Simplified	凿	灿	忧	严	临	痈	肤	导
Traditional	圖	釀	寧	尷	兩	摺	齣	鬱
Draft	啚	酖	宁	尬	両	扟	齣	玉
Simplified	图	酿	宁	尴	两	折	出	郁

The Influence of Chinese Characters

Chinese characters are one of the most significant scripts in the history of the world. The ideographic feature of Chinese characters had enabled people to read the same script although they spoke different languages. Chinese characters used to be the only writing system for official documents in ancient Japan, the Korean Peninsula, Vietnam, the Ryukyu Islands, and The Lanfang Republic, playing an irreplaceable role in the spread of culture and the expansion of trade. The Khitan, Jurchen, the Tangut script, Sawndip, and Bouyei writing were all developed under the influence of Chinese characters, though they died out for different reasons. The tremendous impact of Chinese characters on neighboring cultures once created a cultural area in which Chinese characters circulated as the common script as they were adopted into the writing systems in Japan , the Korean Peninsula, and Vietnam. To this day, Chinese characters still constitute a part of the Japanese writing system.

The front entrance of a temple, a memorial archway, in Ho Chi Minh City, Vietnam

© *xiquinhosilva*

Chinese inscription on the plaque of Namhansanseong in South Korea

© *Khitai*

Tokyo, Japan

© *Francesco Crippa*

Hanging Lantern in the Kek Lok Si Temple in Malaysia

© *Ah Wei (Lung Wei)*

The Influence of Chinese Characters on the Japanese Writing System

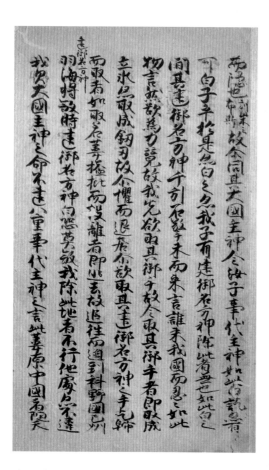

Shinpukuji manuscript of the Kojiki
© Ken'yu, Koten Hozonkai, Wikimedia Commons

Kishu Honmyo Shobu. Volume 1 (Man'yogana)
© National Diet Library

Despite the fact that the culture of the Japanese nation has a long history, the creation of its own writing system was relatively late. Chinese characters had long been used to transmit thoughts and express emotions by the Japanese people. Though as to when Chinese characters were introduced into Japan still remains unknown, it is believed that ancient Japanese served as a spoken language and the introduction of Chinese characters provided a means of writing—script. Recognized as the earliest Japanese record, the *Kojiki* (古事記) (712) was compiled in Chinese characters, called *kanbun* (漢文). Chinese characters had begun to be used to write Japanese phonetically to indicate Japanese words instead of their semantic value by the 8th and 9th Centuries, with the development of *Man'yogana* (万葉仮名). Due to the extensive disparities in syntax and phonology between Chinese and Japanese spoken languages, and the complex nature of *kanji* (adopted logographic Chinese characters used in the Japanese writing system), the two kana systems, hiragana and katakana, were developed independently, with hiragana was derived from the simplified cursive script of Chinese characters, often used by women, and katakana, originating from the radicals of Chinese characters in regular script, was used by Buddhist monks in Japan who inserted these kana beside the kanji to help memorize the Japanese inflections. In Post-World War II, a rapid and significant reform of the writing system was launched, for instance, the issue of *Tōyō kanjihyō* (List of Kanji for General Use) (1946) mandated a collection of 1850 characters for use in schools, textbooks, official documents, and publications. And after 30 years of use, *Jōyō kanji* (Regular-use Chinese Characters), a modification of *Tōyō kanjihyō*, was released with the number of the collection of characters increasing to 1945, which extended to 2136 in 2010.

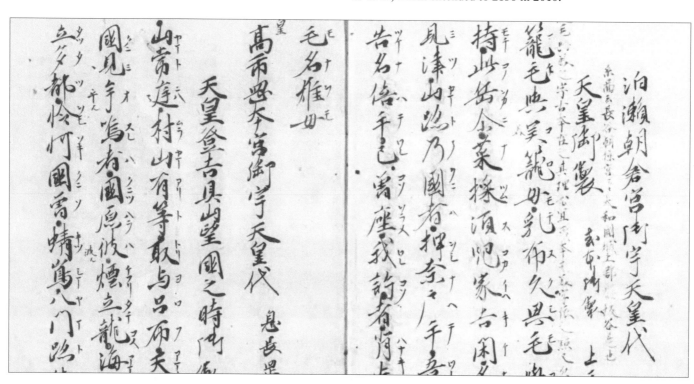

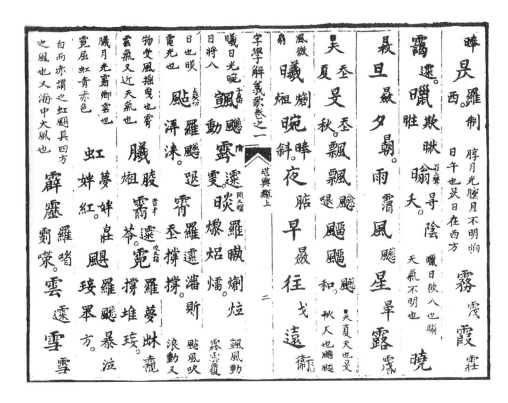

The Chữ Nôm script in the
Dialogues of Cochinchinois printed in 1871

© Wikimedia Commons

The Influence of Chinese Characters on the Vietnamese Writing System

From 207 BC to AD 939, under the direct rule of several Chinese dynasties, Chinese culture had profoundly influenced Vietnam. In the 9th century, Chinese characters called Chữ Nho (scholars' script) was adopted as an official written script for governmental and official documents. Even after Vietnam declared its independence from the rule of ancient China, Chữ Nho still served as a common script among literati, in education and in the creation of literature. A system to write Vietnamese called ChữNôm was developed in the 13th century, created on the basis of Chinese ideographs. The invention of the ChữNôm was by combining Chinese characters and a set of newly created characters to write Vietnamese words. The complexity of the new characters led to their limited use, so Chinese characters were still widely used and remained as the official written script until the early 20th century. But the French colonial authorities launched a tremendous language reform movement starting from the latter half of the 19th century, when the use of Chinese characters was forcibly discouraged and a romanized writing system named Quốcngữ was promoted as the standard script in Vietnam. Since then, no trace of Chinese characters can be found in the Vietnamese writing system. However, due to the deep roots of Chinese culture in Vietnam, it is not difficult to find Chữ- Nho in today's calligraphic banners used on traditional occasions.

*Tự Đức Thánh Chế Tự Học
Giải Nghĩa Ca
(a Chữ Nôm—Chinese Dictionary),
first published in 1898*

© Wikimedia Commons

The Influence of Chinese Characters on the Korean Writing System

나랏말ᄊᆞ미 中國귁에 달아 文문字ᄍᆞ와로 서르 ᄉᆞᄆᆞᆺ디 아니ᄒᆞᆯᄊᆡ 이런 젼ᄎᆞ로 어린 百ᄇᆡᆨ姓셰ᇰ이 니르고져 홇 배 이셔도 ᄆᆞᄎᆞᆷ내 제 ᄠᅳ들 시러 펴디 몯ᄒᆞᇙ 노미 하니라 내 이ᄅᆞᆯ 爲윙ᄒᆞ야 어엿비 너겨 새로 스믈 여듧 字ᄍᆞᄅᆞᆯ ᄆᆡᇰᄀᆞ노니 사ᄅᆞᆷ마다 ᄒᆡᅇᅧ 수ᄫᅵ 니겨 날로 ᄡᅮ메 便뼌安한킈 ᄒᆞ고져 ᄒᆞᇙ ᄯᆞᄅᆞ미니라

Hanja and Old Hangul part of
Hunminjeongeum

During the Samhan era, between the Han dynasty defeat of Gojoseon (108 BC) and the maturation of the Three Kingdoms (Goguryeo, Baekje, and Silla, 57 BC to 668), Chinese characters were introduced to Korea along with Buddhism, known as *hanja*. For a millennium, the Koreans coupled classical Chinese characters primarily with native phonetic scripts such as Idu, Gugyeol, and Hyangchal. This was before the creation of the new Korean alphabet. However, the massive differences between the Korean and Chinese languages contributed to a high illiteracy rate in Korea. An education of hanja was accessible only among privileged elites, leaving many lower-class Koreans illiterate. To improve the situation and solve the problem of the inadequacy of hanja to write in Korean, in the 15th century, King Sejong the Great invented a new Korean alphabet: the writing system known today as Hangul. The project is described in the document *Hunminjeongeum*, published in 1446, according to which the writing system of the newly created alphabet, called *eonmun* (colloquial script), effectively raised the literacy rate among commoners nationwide. However, the privileged elites denounced it as *amkeul* (female script), insisting that hanja should be *jinseo* (true text). In 1894, hanja was replaced by Hangul as Korea's national script, along with the rise of Korean nationalism and the Gabo Reform. Despite the fact that hanja are rarely used in both South Korea and North Korea today, the deep roots of Chinese culture in Korean history determine the indispensable use of Chinese characters to some extent.

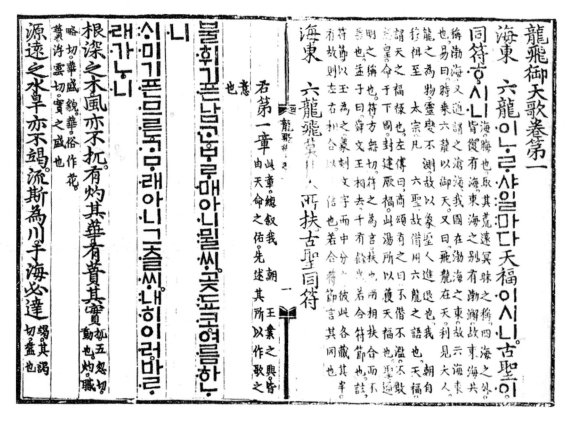

The book
Yongbieocheonga
published in 1447

The Influence of Chinese Characters in Singapore and Malaysia

Chinese and English newspaper in Malaysia
© Valéran Sabourin

Chinese characters are ubiquitous in both Singapore and Malaysia. Though both countries have adopted different policies concerning the Chinese language, they share a similar history regarding the cultural impact of Chinese characters. In the 19th century, to escape war and poverty and to search for better lives, a large number of Chinese laborers known as "coolies" flowed into Singapore and Malaysia from Southern China. They took root and gradually constituted an important population in the demographic composition of both lands. Thus, Chinese became one of the most widely used languages.

After the divorce of Singapore and Malaysia, different policies were implemented. In Singapore, the Simplified Chinese released in mainland China was adopted as the official language and has been used within government ever since. But unlike in mainland China, the use of traditional Chinese characters was not officially regulated and Singaporeans are encouraged to learn both Simplified and Traditional Chinese characters so that they can communicate and do business with Chinese people around the world. Chinese, however, is not an official language in Malaysia. Simplified Chinese is taught in Chinese schools, whereas traditional Chinese is also widely used on signboards and in the titles of articles appearing in Chinese newspapers.

Traditional Chinese and English used in signboard of Chinese restaurant in Singapore
© Michael Coghlan

Simplified Chinese used in ornaments in Singapore
© GillyBerlin

Glyphic Evolution
of 132 Hanzi

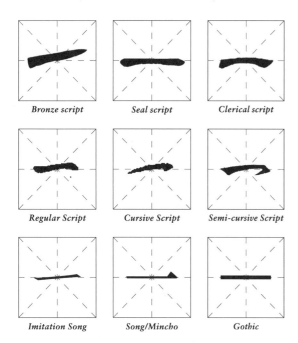

Bronze script   Seal script   Clerical script

Regular Script   Cursive Script   Semi-cursive Script

Imitation Song   Song/Mincho   Gothic

The original meaning of character "一" (one):
the minimum original unit, the smallest positive integer.

◉ *Oracle bone script:*
It is a simple ideogram representing the simplest origin and
the most abundant chaotic whole. There is a saying in *Tao Te
Ching* written by Lao Tsu (571 BC—471 BC), "Tao gave birth
to the One; the One gave birth successively to Two things,
Three things, up to ten thousand."

◉ *Oracle bone script*

The original meaning of character "二" (two):
two polars—heaven and earth.

◉ *Oracle bone script:*
Character "二" (two) is made up of two rightward strokes, the upper
one representing the heaven, the lower one the earth.

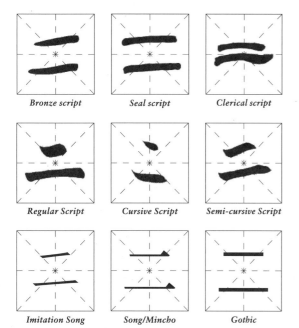

Bronze script   Seal script   Clerical script

Regular Script   Cursive Script   Semi-cursive Script

Imitation Song   Song/Mincho   Gothic

◉ *Oracle bone script*

Bronze script

Seal script

Clerical script

Regular Script

Cursive Script

Semi-cursive Script

Imitation Song

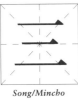
Song/Mincho

Gothic

The original meaning of character "三" (three):
heaven, earth, and men.

◉ *Oracle bone script:*
Character "三" (three) is made up of three rightward strokes, created by adding one more stroke representing "men" to character "二" (two).

◉ *Oracle bone script*

Bronze script

Seal script

Clerical script

Regular Script

Cursive Script

Semi-cursive Script

Imitation Song

Song/Mincho

Gothic

The original meaning of character "四" (four):
a positive integer twice as large as two.

◉ *Oracle bone script:*
It is a simple ideogram composed of four rightward strokes.

◉ *Seal script:*
It is the combination of four vertical strokes and character "二".

◉ *Oracle bone script*

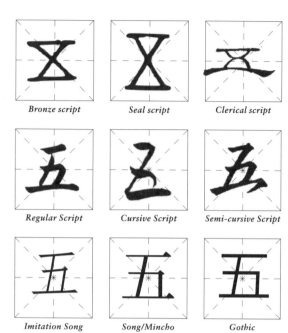

Bronze script | Seal script | Clerical script

Regular Script | Cursive Script | Semi-cursive Script

Imitation Song | Song/Mincho | Gothic

The original meaning of character "五" (five):
the basic elements of the universe: gold, wood, water, fire, and earth.

◉*Oracle bone script:*
It is an ideogram with a cross which suggests that everything is connected in the universe. Some forms have two strokes added above and below the cross to signify everything between the heaven and the earth.

◉*Oracle bone script*

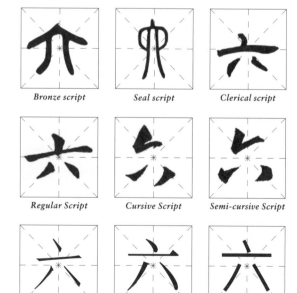

Bronze script | Seal script | Clerical script

Regular Script | Cursive Script | Semi-cursive Script

Imitation Song | Song/Mincho | Gothic

The original meaning of character "六" (six):
a cottage, consisting of four walls, a roof, and ground.

◉*Oracle bone script:*
It resembles the frame of a cottage.

◉*Clerical script:*
The "roof" was simplified into the combination of a dot and a rightward stroke.

◉*Oracle bone script*

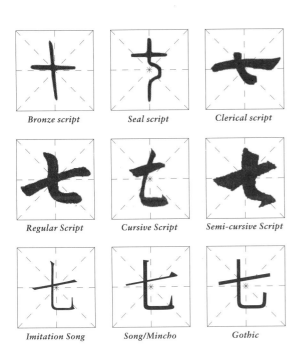

Bronze script	*Seal script*	*Clerical script*
Regular Script	*Cursive Script*	*Semi-cursive Script*
Imitation Song	*Song/Mincho*	*Gothic*

The original meaning of character "七" (seven):
the original character of "切" (to cut), a limit number that the ancient people considered needed to be further subdivided, the positive integer between six and eight.

◉ *Oracle bone script:*
It is a simple ideogram consisting of a rightward stroke representing a whole, and a downward stroke that means dividing the whole.

◉ *Seal script:*
To distinguish from character "十" (ten), the downward stroke in bronze script was transformed into a four-fold turning.

◉ *Clerical script :*
The four-fold turning was transformed into one single turning.

◉ *Oracle bone script*

Bronze script	*Seal script*	*Clerical script*
Regular Script	*Cursive Script*	*Semi-cursive Script*
Imitation Song	*Song/Mincho*	*Gothic*

The original meaning of character "八" (eight):
to part and go in opposite directions.

◉ *Oracle bone script:*
It is a simple ideogram with two opposite arcs symbolizing two separate parts of an object.

◉ *Clerical script:*
The arcs were transformed into a left-falling stroke and a right-falling stroke.

◉ *Oracle bone script*

Bronze script

Seal script

Clerical script

Regular Script

Cursive Script

Semi-cursive Script

Imitation Song

Song/Mincho

Gothic

The original meaning of character "九" (nine):
the original character of "肘" (elbow).

◉*Oracle bone script:*
It resembles human's elbow, but it was subsequently used to represent the number nine.

◉*Oracle bone script*

Bronze script

Seal script

Clerical script

Regular Script

Cursive Script

Semi-cursive Script

Imitation Song

Song/Mincho

Gothic

The original meaning of character "十" (ten):
a rope used to make knots to keep record, representing the total number.

◉*Oracle bone script:*
It is a pictogram, representing a hanging rope used to record by making knots.

◉*Bronze script:*
It was transformed into a simple ideogram with an addition of a dot to the "rope" to indicate record keeping.

◉*Oracle bone script*

Bronze script

Seal script

Clerical script

Regular Script

Cursive Script

Semi-cursive Script

Imitation Song

Song/Mincho

Gothic

The original meaning of character "百" (hundred):
ten tens.

◉ *Oracle bone script:*
It consists of a rightward stroke and the sign "白" which has a similar pronunciation.

◉ *Oracle bone script*

Bronze script

Seal script

Clerical script

Regular Script

Cursive Script

Semi-cursive Script

Imitation Song

Song/Mincho

Gothic

The original meaning of character "千" (thousand):
a unit of quantity describing a great number of people.

◉ *Oracle bone script:*
It is a simple ideogram, composed of a rightward stroke and the sign "人" (people).

◉ *Clerical script*：
The shape of "人" (man) disappeared.

◉ *Oracle bone script*

Traditional
Simplified

Bronze script

Seal script

Clerical script

Regular Script

Cursive Script

Semi-cursive Script

Imitation Song

Song/Mincho

Gothic

The original meaning of character "万" (ten thousand):
a great number of scorpions.

◉ *Oracle bone script:*
It resembles the shape of a cuspidal scorpion with big chelae and a tail. (In the ancient times, there is a huge number of scorpions in the Central Plains, so scorpions were used to represent a huge number.)

◉ *Bronze script:*
The sign of a hand was added,
to signify the act of catching scorpions.

◉ *Regular script:*
The shape of two hands was changed into "艹".
The simplified form is composed of the sign "人"
and a rightward stroke, meaning that a great
number of people cluster together in a place.
There is an assumption that it evolved from the
symbol "卍", meaning eternity.

▲ **Simplified Character:**
The simplified character "万" is
the simplified form in regular script.

◉ *Oracle bone script*

Bronze script

Seal script

Clerical script

Regular Script

Cursive Script

Semi-cursive Script

Imitation Song

Song/Mincho

Gothic

The original meaning of character "兽" (beast):
to lie in ambush to hunt, along with a hound and stones
used as weapons.

◉ *Oracle bone script:*
It consists of "單" (a weapon made of twig and stones)
and the sign of a hound.

◉ *Seal script:*
The component "單" was changed into the inexplicable "嘼".

◉ *Clerical script:*
The "嘼" was simplified.

▲ **Simplified Character:**
In the simplified character "兽",
the component "犬" was omitted,
and the two "口" were simplified
into two dots according to the
rules of cursive script.

◉ *Oracle bone script*

Bronze script

Seal script

Clerical script

Regular Script

Cursive Script

Semi-cursive Script

Imitation Song

Song/Mincho

Gothic

The original meaning of character "凤" (phoenix):
a legendary divine bird for the worshiping of God, with a gorgeous crown and long tail feather, also known as the king of birds.

◉ *Oracle bone script:*
It resembles the shape of a phoenix.

◉ *Seal script:*
It is the combination of the signs "凡" and "鳥" (bird).

▲Simplified Character:
In the simplified character "凤", "鳥" was replaced by "又" based on the form in cursive script.

◉ *Oracle bone script*

Bronze script

Seal script

Clerical script

Regular Script

Cursive Script

Semi-cursive Script

Imitation Song

Song/Mincho

Gothic

The original meaning of character "鸟" (bird):
a flying creature with a long tail.

◉ *Oracle bone script:*
It resembles a bird with a beak, feather and claws.

◉ *Seal script:*
The shape of the beak faded, and the "claws" were simplified into "匕".

◉ *Clerical script:*
The "tail feather" was transformed into four dots "灬", leading to the disappearance of the vivid image of a bird.

▲Simplified Character:
In the simplified character "鸟", the four dots were replaced by a rightward stroke based on the rules of cursive script.

◉ *Oracle bone script*

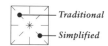
Traditional

Simplified

Bronze script

Seal script

Clerical script

Regular Script

Cursive Script

Semi-cursive Script

Imitation Song

Song/Mincho

Gothic

The original meaning of character "龙" (dragon):
a mythical creature with horns and a big mouth full of sharp teeth.

◉ *Oracle bone script:*
The sign "辛" (instrument of torture, meaning that dragon is the king of animals) was added to the head of the creature.

◉ *Seal script:*
"匕" and "彡" were added to the body of the creature, representing the sharp claws and fins .

◉ *Clerical script:*
"辛"was replaced by "立".

▲Simplified Character:
In the simplified character "龙", the left part ("立" and "月") in the traditional character was removed and the form in cursive script was adopted as a complete character.

◉ *Oracle bone script*

Bronze script

Seal script

Clerical script

Regular Script

Cursive Script

Semi-cursive Script

Imitation Song

Song/Mincho

Gothic

The original meaning of character "牛" (cattle):
a mammal with strong body and curved horns, capable of plowing field and pulling cart.

◉ *Oracle bone script:*
It resembles the head of a cattle, emphasizing the V-shaped nose as well as a pair of protruding horns.

◉ *Clerical script:*
The curvy lines were turned straight.

◉ *Oracle bone script*

Bronze script

Seal script

Clerical script

Regular Script

Cursive Script

Semi-cursive Script

Imitation Song

Song/Mincho

Gothic

The original meaning of character "犬" (dog):
a good helper of watching over house and hunting

◉ *Oracle bone script:*
It resembles a dog.

◉ *Seal script:*
The shape of a dog disappeared.

◉ *Clerical script:*
It is the combination of character "大" (big) and a dot.

◉ *Oracle bone script*

Bronze script

Seal script

Clerical script

Regular Script

Cursive Script

Semi-cursive Script

Imitation Song

Song/Mincho

Gothic

The original meaning of character "兔" (rabbit):
a docile herbivorous mammal.

◉ *Oracle bone script:*
It resembles the shape of a rabbit with an open mouth,
a short tail, and a pair of long ears.

◉ *Seal script:*
The sign "口" (mouth) was turned into "刀", and "目" was
placed horizontally, leading to the disappearance of the vivid
image of a rabbit.

◉ *Clerical script:*
The "leg" was stylized into a turning and a dot.

◉ *Oracle bone script*

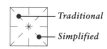

Traditional

Simplified

Bronze script

Seal script

Clerical script

Regular Script

Cursive Script

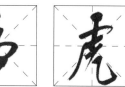

Semi-cursive Script

Imitation Song

Song/Mincho

Gothic

The original meaning of character "虎" (tiger):
the king of animals in mountain that would attack humans.

◉*Oracle bone script:*
It resembles a tiger with a big mouth, long legs, and stripes.

◉*Seal script:*
The sign of the tail was changed to "人" (human), meaning
that tigers would attack humans.

◉*Oracle bone script*

Bronze script

Seal script

Clerical script

Regular Script

Cursive Script

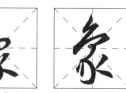

Semi-cursive Script

Imitation Song

Song/Mincho

Gothic

The original meaning of character "象" (elephant):
a herbivore with a long nose and a large body.

◉*Oracle bone script:*
It resembles an elephant but vertically placed.

◉*Seal script:*
The sign of the long nose was changed to "人".

◉*Oracle bone script*

Bronze script

Seal script

Clerical script

Regular Script

Cursive Script

Semi-cursive Script

Imitation Song

Song/Mincho

Gothic

The original meaning of character "鹿" (deer):
a ruminant with four long thin legs and a short tail.
A male one usually grows branching horns called antlers.

◉ *Oracle bone script:*
It resembles a deer with big eyes, antlers, and a short tail.

◉ *Seal script:*
The shape of the antlers faded, whereas the shape
of the hooves was emphasized.

◉ *Clerical script:*
The shape of the antlers disappeared.

◉ *Oracle bone script*

Bronze script

Seal script

Clerical script

Regular Script

Cursive Script

Semi-cursive Script

Imitation Song

Song/Mincho

Gothic

The original meaning of character "鱼" (fish):
a cold-blooded aquatic vertebrate in streamlined shape
with fins and gills.

◉ *Oracle bone script:*
It resembles a fish with an open mouth.

◉ *Seal script:*
The sign of the fish tail was simplified into "火".

◉ *Clerical script:*
"火" was changed to four dots "灬".

▲ **Simplified Character:**
In the simplified character "鱼", the four dots were changed
to a rightward stroke according to the rules of cursive script.

◉ *Oracle bone script*

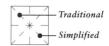

Bronze script

Seal script

Clerical script

Regular Script

Cursive Script

Semi-cursive Script

Imitation Song

Song/Mincho

Gothic

The original meaning of character "马" (horse):
a strong animal good at running.

◉ *Oracle bone script:*
It resembles a horse with flying mane, a long tail, hooves,
and a big eye that represents the head.

◉ *Seal script:*
The shapes of the eye, mane, legs, and tail were simplified.

◉ *Clerical script:*
The signs of two hooves and the tail were changed into four
dots "灬" and a turning stroke respectively.

▲ Simplified Character:
In the simplified character "马",
the four dots were changed to
a rightward stroke according to
the rules of cursive script.

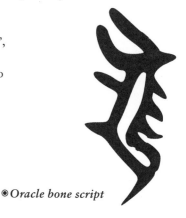

◉ *Oracle bone script*

Bronze script

Seal script

Clerical script

Regular Script

Cursive Script

Semi-cursive Script

Imitation Song

Song/Mincho

Gothic

The original meaning of character "鸡" (chicken):
a peacock-like bird that was caught from the woods
and got domesticated.

◉ *Oracle bone script:*
It resembles a cock with its feet tied with a rope.

◉ *Seal script:*
It is a phono-semantic compound, with "奚" as the phonetic
indicator and "鳥"(bird) as the semantic indicator.

▲ Simplified Character:
In the simplified character "鸡",
according to the principle of Simplification by Analogy*,
the complicated "奚" was replaced by "又" (to catch).

*Simplification by Analogy is a principle
adopted in the *Table of General Standard
Chinese Characters*. It requires that, in most
cases, a simplified character retains its form
when it constitutes a part of other characters.

◉ *Oracle bone script*

Bronze script

Seal script

Clerical script

Regular Script

Cursive Script

Semi-cursive Script

Imitation Song

Song/Mincho

Gothic

The original meaning of character "羊" (goat):
a docile herbivore with two curved horns.

◉ *Oracle bone script:*
It resembles a head of an animal with two curved horns and a V-shaped nose. There is another form with a short horizontal stroke added between the horns and the nose.

◉ *Oracle bone script*

Bronze script

Seal script

Clerical script

Regular Script

Cursive Script

Semi-cursive Script

Imitation Song

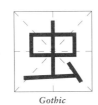
Song/Mincho

Gothic

The original meaning of character "虫" (worm):
the original character of "蛇"(snake).

◉ *Oracle bone script:*
It resembles a snake with a rounded head and long body.

◉ *Seal script:*
The shape of the head was exaggerated.

◉ *Oracle bone script*

Traditional
Simplified

Bronze script

Seal script

Clerical script

Regular Script

Cursive Script

Semi-cursive Script

Imitation Song

Song/Mincho

Gothic

The original meaning of character "贝" (shell):
an aquatic mollusk with calcareous hard shell.

◉ *Oracle bone script:*
It resembles a shellfish, but some other forms have
horizontal strokes that represent the stripes on the shell.

◉ *Bronze script:*
The symmetrical feature of bivalve mollusk was emphasized.

▲ Simplified Character:
In the simplified character "贝", the two rightward strokes
were omitted based on the form in cursive script.

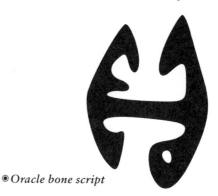
◉ *Oracle bone script*

Bronze script

Seal script

Clerical script

Regular Script

Cursive Script

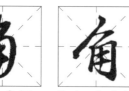
Semi-cursive Script

Imitation Song

Song/Mincho

Gothic

The original meaning of character "角" (horn):
the hard pointed projection on the heads of some animals
such as bulls or deers.

◉ *Oracle bone script:*
It resembles a horn.

◉ *Bronze script:*
The sign of buckle was added to the top of the horn.

◉ *Seal script:*
The "buckle" was changed to the sign "人".

◉ *Oracle bone script*

Bronze script

Seal script

Clerical script

Regular Script

Cursive Script

Semi-cursive Script

Imitation Song

Song/Mincho

Gothic

The original meaning of character "尾" (tail):
a fake tail worn by people as imitation of animals,
when they dance or celebrate.

◉ *Oracle bone script:*
It depicts a man with a hanging hairy tail-like
attachment.

◉ *Clerical script:*
It is a combination of "尸" and "毛".

◉ *Oracle bone script*

Bronze script

Seal script

Clerical script

Regular Script

Cursive Script

Semi-cursive Script

Imitation Song

Song/Mincho

Gothic

The original meaning of character "稻" (rice):
to crush grain with a stone mortar, and then toss it in the air in
order to separate the rice from the chaff.

◉ *Oracle bone script:*
The upper part is the rice that is tossed in the air, while the lower
part resembles a bamboo basket of grain .

◉ *Bronze script:*
It is a phono-semantic compound, with semantic indicator "禾"
on the left and phonetic indicator "舀" on the right.

◉ *Oracle bone script*

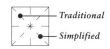

Bronze script

Seal script

Clerical script

Regular Script

Cursive Script

Semi-cursive Script

Imitation Song

Song/Mincho

Gothic

The original meaning of character "麦" (wheat):
a crop introduced from foreign countries.

◉ *Oracle bone script:*
It evolved from character "來" (to come) which carries the features of root, stem and leaves. "夂" as the lower part resembles feet, which might suggest the foreign origin of the plant .

▲**Simplified Character:**
The simplified character "麦" is from the form in clerical script.

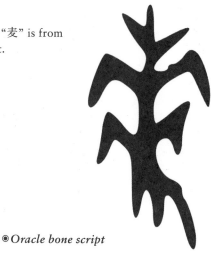

◉ *Oracle bone script*

Bronze script

Seal script

Clerical script

Regular Script

Cursive Script

Semi-cursive Script

Imitation Song

Song/Mincho

Gothic

The original meaning of character "草" (grass):
the grass that newly sprout.

◉ *Oracle bone script:*
It resembles a bud with leaves.

◉ *Bronze script:*
It consists of "艸" (grass) and the original character of "早" .

◉ *Seal script:*
The four signs of grass were reduced to two.

◉ *Clerical script:*
The "艸" was changed into "艹".

◉ *Oracle bone script*

Bronze script

Seal script

Clerical script

Regular Script

Cursive Script

Semi-cursive Script

Imitation Song

Song/Mincho

Gothic

The original meaning of character "禾" (grain): ripe crop.

◉ *Oracle bone script:*
It resembles a droopy crop.

◉ *Oracle bone script*

Bronze script

Seal script

Clerical script

Regular Script

Cursive Script

Semi-cursive Script

Imitation Song

Song/Mincho

Gothic

The original meaning of character "树" (tree): to plant.

◉ *Oracle bone script:*
It consists of signs of a small plant, a container, and a grabbing hand, representing the act of putting a plantlet in a pot.

◉ *Bronze script:*
The small plant on top was changed to "屮" (grass).

◉ *Seal script:*
The sign "木" (wood) was added.

◉ *Clerical script:*
The sign of the hand on the right was changed to "寸".

▲Simplified Character:
In the simplified character "树", the middle part was simplified into "又", based on the form in cursive script.

◉ *Oracle bone script*

Bronze script

Seal script

Clerical script

Regular Script

Cursive Script

Semi-cursive Script

Imitation Song

Song/Mincho

Gothic

The original meaning of character "果" (fruit):
the part of a plant that contains seeds.

◉*Oracle bone script:*
It resembles a woody plant with three ripe fruits.

◉*Bronze script:*
The three fruits were reduced to one, depicted with seeds inside.

◉*Seal script:*
The shape of the seeds was simplified into "田".

◉*Clerical script:*
The lower part was simplified into "木".

◉*Oracle bone script*

Bronze script

Seal script

Clerical script

Regular Script

Cursive Script

Semi-cursive Script

Imitation Song

Song/Mincho

Gothic

The original meaning of character "栗" (chestnut):
thorny fruits.

◉*Oracle bone script:*
It resembles a tree full of thorny fruits.

◉*Bronze script:*
The shape of the thorns faded.

◉*Seal script:*
The upper part was changed to "西".

◉*Oracle bone script*

Bronze script

Seal script

Clerical script

Regular Script

Cursive Script

Semi-cursive Script

Imitation Song

Song/Mincho

Gothic

The original meaning of character "竹" (bamboo):
bamboo with hollow stem, nodes and shoots.

◉ *Bronze script:*
It resembles two bamboo stems with leaves.

◉ *Clerical script:*
It was simplified into the combination of two "个".

◉ *Oracle bone script*

Bronze script

Seal script

Clerical script

Regular Script

Cursive Script

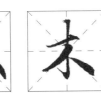

Semi-cursive Script

Imitation Song

Song/Mincho

Gothic

The original meaning of character "木" (wood):
trees.

◉ *Oracle bone script:*
It resembles a tree with branches and roots.

◉ *Clerical script:*
The vivid image of a tree disappeared by turning lines into strokes.

◉ *Oracle bone script*

Bronze script

Seal script

Clerical script

Regular Script

Cursive Script

Semi-cursive Script

Imitation Song

Song/Mincho

Gothic

The original meaning of character "春" (spring):
the time when everything revives after the cold winter.

◉*Oracle bone script:*
It consists of "林" (woods), "日" (sun),
and "屯" (to sprout).

◉*Bronze script:*
The three components were simplified, with "林" changed
into "艸" (grass).

◉*Clerical script:*
The "艸" and "屯" were combined.

◉*Oracle bone script*

Bronze script

Seal script

Clerical script

Regular Script

Cursive Script

Semi-cursive Script

Imitation Song

Song/Mincho

Gothic

The original meaning of character "冬" (winter):
the original character of "终" (end), meaning the end of a rope record.

◉*Oracle bone script:*
It resembles a rope with two knots for record at both ends, indicating the
end of keeping records.

◉*Bronze script:*
The two knots were moved to the middle and the sign "日" (sun) was
added to signify an end of a cycle.

◉*Seal script:*
The "日" was omitted; "仌" (ice) was added to stress the icy winter.

◉*Clerical script:*
The upper part was changed to "夂", and "仌"
was simplified into two dots.

◉*Oracle bone script*

Bronze script

Seal script

Clerical script

Regular Script

Cursive Script

Semi-cursive Script

Imitation Song

Song/Mincho

Gothic

The original meaning of character "夏" (summer):
the capable Chinese people.

◉1—Bronze script:
It consists of "頁" (head), the signs of hands and "止" (foot),
indicating a capable man.

◉Seal script:
The signs of "止" were replaced by "夊".

◉Regular script:
The signs of hands were omitted and the whole
character was simplified.

Bronze script

Seal script

Clerical script

Regular Script

Cursive Script

Semi-cursive Script

Imitation Song

Song/Mincho

Gothic

The original meaning of character "秋" (autumn):
the season when the weather gets cool and crickets sing.

◉Oracle bone script:
It resembles a cricket with long legs and tentacles.

◉Bronze script:
On the left is a circle above "火" (fire, indicating the burning wheat
straw), indicating the burning wheat straw), and on the right is the
sign "禾"(rice plant).

◉Seal script:
The circle was omitted.

◉Oracle bone script

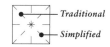

Bronze script

Seal script

Clerical script

Regular Script

Cursive Script

Semi-cursive Script

Imitation Song

Song/Mincho

Gothic

The original meaning of character "寒" (cold):
to use paillasse to keep warm during the freezing cold nights.

◉ *Oracle bone script:*
It consists of "宀" (bedroom), "人" (man), and
four dots which represent the paillasse.

◉ *Bronze script:*
It consists of: "宀", "茻"(paillasse), "人",
"夕" (evening), and "二" (which represents the ice).

◉ *Seal script:*
The "夕" was omitted, while "二" was changed
to "仌" to stress the freezing weather.

◉ *Clerical script:*
The "茻" was changed to "井", "人" to
"大", and "仌" to two dots.

◉ *Oracle bone script*

Bronze script

Seal script

Clerical script

Regular Script

Cursive Script

Semi-cursive Script

Imitation Song

Song/Mincho

Gothic

The original meaning of character "湿" (humid):
the wet silk cloth hanging on a rack.

◉ *Oracle bone script:*
On the left is the sign of water, while on the right is the
hanging silk cloth.

◉ *Bronze script:*
The sign "土" (earth) was added to indicate that the silk cloth gets
damped on the ground.

◉ *Seal script:*
"土" was omitted and "日"(sun) was added to emphasize the drying
of the silk cloth.

◉ *Clerical script:*
The sign of water was simplified into "氵".

▲Simplified Character:
The simplified character "湿"
is based on the vulgar form
in regular script.

◉ *Oracle bone script*

Bronze script

Seal script

Clerical script

Regular Script

Cursive Script

Semi-cursive Script

Imitation Song

Song/Mincho

Gothic

The original meaning of character "阳" (sun):
the south-facing side of a mountain.

◉*Oracle bone script:*
It combines the signs "阜" (hill) and "昜" (sunshine).

◉*Bronze script:*
"彡" (shadow) was added to "昜", referring to the shadow
caused by sunlight.

◉*Clerical script:*
The "阜" was changed to "阝".

▲**Simplified Character:**
In the simplified character "阳",
"昜" was replaced by "日" (sun).

◉*Oracle bone script*

Bronze script

Seal script

Clerical script

Regular Script

Cursive Script

Semi-cursive Script

Imitation Song

Song/Mincho

Gothic

The original meaning of character "月" (moon):
the planet whose cycle of phases can be observed in the night sky.

◉*Oracle bone script:*
It consists of a semicircle (the moon) and a short downward
stroke inside (indicating the glowing feature of the moon).

◉*Seal script:*
The shape of the semicircle was changed.

◉*Oracle bone script*

Bronze script

Seal script

Clerical script

Regular Script

Cursive Script

Semi-cursive Script

Imitation Song

Song/Mincho

Gothic

The original meaning of character "星" (star): the luminous objects scattered in the night sky.

◉*Oracle bone script:*
It is composed of five circles (many stars), and the sign "生"(to grow).

◉*Bronze script:*
The five circles were changed into three "日".

◉*Seal script:*
The three "日" were reduced to one.

◉*Clerical script:*
The sign "生" was further changed.

◉*Oracle bone script*

Bronze script

Seal script

Clerical script

Regular Script

Cursive Script

Semi-cursive Script

Imitation Song

Song/Mincho

Gothic

The original meaning of character "火" (fire): flame.

◉*Oracle bone script:*
It resembles the flames on ground with its shape similar to character "山".

◉*Bronze script:*
The "flames" were reduced into one, with the addition of two dots representing the sparkles around the fire.

◉*Oracle bone script*

Bronze script

Seal script

Clerical script

Regular Script

Cursive Script

Semi-cursive Script

Imitation Song

Song/Mincho

Gothic

The original meaning of character"雨"(rain):
the water falling from sky.

◉ *Oracle bone script:*
The horizontal stroke above represents the sky while the lower part signifies the falling rain drops.

◉ *Oracle bone script*

Bronze script

Seal script

Clerical script

Regular Script

Cursive Script

Semi-cursive Script

Imitation Song

Song/Mincho

Gothic

The original meaning of character "雷" (thunder):
the loud noise caused by lightning.

◉ *Oracle bone script:*
It is composed of two circles (representing the thunder)
and a curvy line (representing the lightening).

◉ *Bronze script:*
The circles were transformed into "田" (resembling wheels)
to emphasize the loud thunder. The sign "雨"(rain) was added
above to show that thunder usually occurs in rainy days.

◉ *Regular script:*
The "畾" was simplified into "田".

◉ *Oracle bone script*

Bronze script

Seal script

Clerical script

Regular Script

Cursive Script

Semi-cursive Script

Imitation Song

Song/Mincho

Gothic

The original meaning of character "皇" (emperor): a king wearing a gold crown.

◉*Oracle bone script:*
It combines the shapes of a shining crown and a big battle axe (the symbol of supreme commander).

◉*Bronze script:*
The shape of the shining crown was simplified and the "battle axe" was changed into "士".

◉*Seal script:*
The sign of crown was changed into "自", while "士" into "王".

◉*Clerical script:*
The "自" was changed into "白".

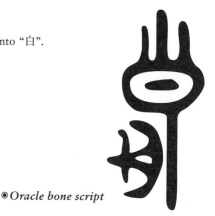
◉*Oracle bone script*

Bronze script

Seal script

Clerical script

Regular Script

Cursive Script

Semi-cursive Script

Imitation Song

Song/Mincho

Gothic

The original meaning of character "民" (people): the prisoners of war who were stabbed in the eye.

◉*Oracle bone script:*
It consists of the signs of an eye and "十"(to hold).

◉*Bronze script:*
The part of eye was made hollow to emphasize the blindness.

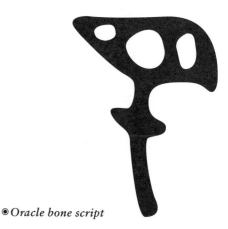
◉*Oracle bone script*

Bronze script

Seal script

Clerical script

Regular Script

Cursive Script

Semi-cursive Script

Imitation Song

Song/Mincho

Gothic

The original meaning of character "童" (child):
the young slaves captured in battles who had been blinded but were trusted because of their innocence.

◉ *Oracle bone script:*
It consists of "辛" (to torture), "目" (eye), and "壬" (to give tasks to a blind slave).

◉ *Bronze script:*
"東" (pack) was added between "目" and "壬", indicating that the young slaves were responsible for taking care of packs during business trip.

◉ *Clerical script:*
The "辛" was changed to "立", whereas "東" and "土" were combined into "里".

◉ *Oracle bone script*

Bronze script

Seal script

Clerical script

Regular Script

Cursive Script

Semi-cursive Script

Imitation Song

Song/Mincho

Gothic

The original meaning of character "女" (female):
unmarried women.

◉ *Oracle bone script:*
It resembles a girl sitting on heels quietly.

◉ *Bronze script:*
A rightward stroke was added above to indicate a hairpin.

◉ *Clerical script:*
The shapes of the girl and her hands faded.

◉ *Oracle bone script*

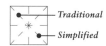

Traditional
Simplified

Bronze script

Seal script

Clerical script

Regular Script

Cursive Script

Semi-cursive Script

Imitation Song

Song/Mincho

Gothic

The original meaning of character "夫" (husband): an adult male.

◉ *Oracle bone script:*
A rightward stroke was added to the "head" of a man to represent a hairpin that signifies adulthood in ancient times.

◉ *Oracle bone script*

Bronze script

Seal script

Clerical script

Regular Script

Cursive Script

Semi-cursive Script

Imitation Song

Song/Mincho

Gothic

The original meaning of character "子" (child): an infant wrapped in cloth.

◉ *Oracle bone script:*
It resembles an infant wrapped in cloth with his arms waving.

◉ *Clerical script:*
It resembles an infant with his arms stretching out.

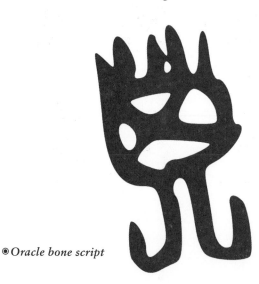

◉ *Oracle bone script*

Bronze script

Seal script

Clerical script

Regular Script

Cursive Script

Semi-cursive Script

Imitation Song

Song/Mincho

Gothic

The original meaning of character "儿" (son): young child.

◉*Oracle bone script:*
It is the combination of "臼" (the unfused skull bones of baby) and "人" (man).

▲Simplified Character:
In the simplified character "儿", the "臼" was omitted.

◉*Oracle bone script*

Bronze script

Seal script

Clerical script

Regular Script

Cursive Script

Semi-cursive Script

Imitation Song

Song/Mincho

Gothic

The original meaning of character "弟" (younger brother): the sequence formed by the enwinding rope on the wooden handle of a weapon.

◉*Oracle bone script:*
It looks like a rope winding around a stake (弋).

◉*Clerical script:*
The shape of "弋" faded.

◉*Oracle bone script*

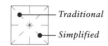

Bronze script

Seal script

Clerical script

Regular Script

Cursive Script

Semi-cursive Script

Imitation Song

Song/Mincho

Gothic

The original meaning of character "王" (king):
the highest ruler of mankind.

◉*Oracle bone script:*
It resembles a huge axe with wide blade and handle.
Some forms have a rightward stroke added.

◉*Oracle bone script*

Bronze script

Seal script

Clerical script

Regular Script

Cursive Script

Semi-cursive Script

Imitation Song

Song/Mincho

Gothic

The original meaning of character "国" (country):
a territory with an independent military and political system
guarded by armed forces.

◉*Oracle bone script:*
It is the combination of the signs "戈" (military force) and "口"
(city walls), indicating the guarded domains.

◉*Bronze script:*
The "或" (domain) was placed in "口".

▲**Simplified Character:**
In the simplified character "国", the inner part was changed from
"或" to "玉" (a dot was added to character "王" to signify that all
territories belong to the king).

◉*Oracle bone script*

Bronze script

Seal script

Clerical script

Regular Script

Cursive Script

Semi-cursive Script

Imitation Song

Song/Mincho

Gothic

The original meaning of character "工" (craft):
a multifunctional ironware.

◉ *Oracle bone script:*
It resembles a multi-purpose tool of ancient craftsman,
with the shape of "T" on one end and
a circle on the other.

◉ *Bronze script:*
It consists of a T shape and a sign of shovel.

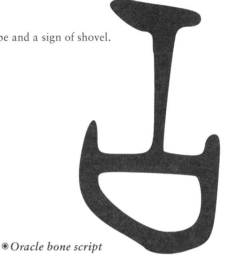

◉ *Oracle bone script*

Bronze script

Seal script

Clerical script

Regular Script

Cursive Script

Semi-cursive Script

Imitation Song

Song/Mincho

Gothic

The original meaning of character "农" (farming):
to weed and plough in the field.

◉ *Oracle bone script:*
It is the combination of the signs of woods and "辰" (a farming tool).

◉ *Bronze script:*
Some forms inherited elements from the oracle bone script; some
had "田" (farmland) added to indicate the cultivating of farmland.

◉ *Seal script:*
It was formed by the combination of several forms in bronze script.

▲**Simplified Character:**
The simplified character "农" is based
on the form in cursive script.

◉ *Oracle bone script*

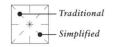

Bronze script

Seal script

Clerical script

Regular Script

Cursive Script

Semi-cursive Script

Imitation Song

Song/Mincho

Gothic

The original meaning of character "军" (army):
the opposing armies have the same number of chariots.

◉*Bronze script:*
It consists of "匀" (equal) and "車" (chariot).

◉*Clerical script:*
The "勺" was changed into "冖".

▲Simplified Character:
In the simplified character "军", "車" was simplified into
"车" according to the law of Simplification by Analogy *in
Complete List of Simplified Characters.*

Bronze script

Seal script

Clerical script

Regular Script

Cursive Script

Semi-cursive Script

Imitation Song

Song/Mincho

Gothic

The original meaning of character "兵" (soldier):
a weapon.

◉*Oracle bone script:*
It consists of the signs of two hands and an axe, indicating
that the warriors fight with battleaxes in hand.

◉*Bronze script:*
The sign of the axe was changed into "斤".

◉*Clerical script:*
The shape of two hands was simplified.

◉*Oracle bone script*

Bronze script

Seal script

Clerical script

Regular Script

Cursive Script

Semi-cursive Script

Imitation Song

Song/Mincho

Gothic

The original meaning of character "官" (official):
the military and political building where a seal authorized
by the court was placed.

◉ *Oracle bone script:*
It is the combination of signs of a house and a commander's seal.

◉ *Oracle bone script*

Bronze script

Seal script

Clerical script

Regular Script

Cursive Script

Semi-cursive Script

Imitation Song

Song/Mincho

Gothic

The original meaning of character "邦" (state):
the domains surrounded by plants.

◉ *Oracle bone script:*
It consists of the signs "丰" (lush trees) and "田"
(boundary, the same as "界").

◉ *Bronze script:*
The character was simplified into "丰"; "邑" (town)
was added to emphasize the idea of domain.

◉ *Clerical script:*
The "邑" was changed into "阝".

◉ *Oracle bone script*

Bronze script

Seal script

Clerical script

Regular Script

Cursive Script

Semi-cursive Script

Imitation Song

Song/Mincho

Gothic

The original meaning of character "人" (human): laborer.

◉*Oracle bone script:*
It resembles a bowing figure.

◉*Oracle bone script*

Bronze script

Seal script

Clerical script

Regular Script

Cursive Script

Semi-cursive Script

Imitation Song

Song/Mincho

Gothic

The original meaning of character "臣" (an official in feudal society): to bow down and receive orders from the emperor.

◉*Oracle bone script:*
It is a vertically placed "目" (eye), indicating obedience.

◉*Seal script:*
The shape of the eye was altered.

◉*Oracle bone script*

Bronze script

Seal script

Clerical script

Regular Script

Cursive Script

Semi-cursive Script

Imitation Song

Song/Mincho

Gothic

The original meaning of character "奴" (slave):
to capture and enslave a woman.

◉ *Oracle bone script:*
It is the combination of "女" (female) and "又" (to catch).

◉ *Oracle bone script*

Bronze script

Seal script

Clerical script

Regular Script

Cursive Script

Semi-cursive Script

Imitation Song

Song/Mincho

Gothic

The original meaning of character "妻" (wife):
a female spouse who is responsible for housework.

◉ *Oracle bone script:*
It is the combination of the signs "女" (female) and "又"
(hand, to comb hair and do housework).

◉ *Bronze script:*
It is the combination of the signs of a hair bun and "母" (mother).

◉ *Oracle bone script*

Bronze script

Seal script

Clerical script

Regular Script

Cursive Script

Semi-cursive Script

Imitation Song

Song/Mincho

Gothic

The original meaning of character "母" (mother): a woman that gives birth and breastfeeds.

◉ *Oracle bone script:*
Two dots were added to character "女" (female) to represent women's breasts for breastfeeding .

◉ *Oracle bone script*

Bronze script

Seal script

Clerical script

Regular Script

Cursive Script

Semi-cursive Script

Imitation Song

Song/Mincho

Gothic

The original meaning of character "男" (male): male laborer who works in the fields.

◉ *Oracle bone script:*
It is the combination of the signs "田" (field) and "力" (physical strength).

◉ *Seal script:*
The sign "力" was transformed into "巾".

◉ *Clerical script:*
The sign "巾" was transformed into "力".

◉ *Oracle bone script*

Bronze script

Seal script

Clerical script

Regular Script

Cursive Script

Semi-cursive Script

Imitation Song

Song/Mincho

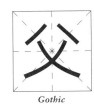

Gothic

The original meaning of character "父" (father):
a parent who educates his children.

◉ *Oracle bone script:*
A downward stroke was added to character "又" (to catch),
showing that a parent educates his children with a stick in hand.

◉ *Clerical script:*
The "又" was changed into a cross.

◉ *Oracle bone script*

Bronze script

Seal script

Clerical script

Regular Script

Cursive Script

Semi-cursive Script

Imitation Song

Song/Mincho

Gothic

The original meaning of character "祖" (ancestor):
offering sacrifices to the ancestors and dividing the meat
into equal shares in rituals.

◉ *Oracle bone script:*
It is a simple ideogram, with the two horizontal strokes inside
meaning that the meat is divided evenly.

◉ *Bronze script:*
The sign "示" (sacrifice) was added.

◉ *Regular script:*
The "示" was simplified into "礻".

◉ *Oracle bone script*

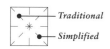
Traditional
Simplified

Bronze script

Seal script

Clerical script

Regular Script

Cursive Script

Semi-cursive Script

Imitation Song

Song/Mincho

Gothic

The original meaning of character "妹" (younger sister):
the younger sister.

◉*Oracle bone script:*
It consists of the signs of a kneeling woman and
the phonetic indicator "未".

◉*Bronze script:*
The character was simplified and the position of the
two parts was switched.

◉*Clerical script:*
The sign "女"(female) was simplified.

◉*Oracle bone script*

Bronze script

Seal script

Clerical script

Regular Script

Cursive Script

Semi-cursive Script

Imitation Song

Song/Mincho

Gothic

The original meaning of character "商" (commerce):
to burn incense for the worship of gods.

◉*Oracle bone script:*
It consists of the signs of burning incense and an altar.

◉*Bronze script:*
"口" was added below.

◉*Oracle bone script*

Bronze script

Seal script

Clerical script

Regular Script

Cursive Script

Semi-cursive Script

Imitation Song

Song/Mincho

Gothic

The original meaning of character "师" (teacher):
a unit of two thousand and five hundred soldiers.

◉ *Oracle bone script:*
It is a sign of two irregular splits of the commander's seal
(used for verification of military power).

◉ *Bronze script:*
The sign of a hat decoration made of animal tail (the symbol of
power) was added, forming the shape of "不".

◉ *Seal script:*
A dot was added to "㠯"; "不" was changed to "帀".

▲ **Simplified Character:**
In the simplified character "师", the left part
was simplified based on the form in cursive script.

◉ *Oracle bone script*

Bronze script

Seal script

Clerical script

Regular Script

Cursive Script

Semi-cursive Script

Imitation Song

Song/Mincho

Gothic

The original meaning of character "旅" (brigade):
a unit of five hundred soldiers.

◉ *Oracle bone script:*
It consists of the sign of a flag and "从" (to follow),
meaning that the soldiers follow, the flying battle flag.

◉ *Clerical script:*
The "从" in seal script was changed to the combination
of "方" and "人".

◉ *Oracle bone script*

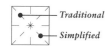
Traditional
Simplified

Bronze script

Seal script

Clerical script

Regular Script

Cursive Script

Semi-cursive Script

Imitation Song

Song/Mincho

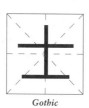
Gothic

The original meaning of character "士" (noncommissioned officer): reputed men in ancient times.

◉ *Oracle bone script:*
It is the combination of "十" (ten) and "一" (one), meaning that a man is capable of doing things and sees them through to the end.

◉ *Bronze script:*
It resembles an axe.

◉ *Oracle bone script*

Bronze script

Seal script

Clerical script

Regular Script

Cursive Script

Semi-cursive Script

Imitation Song

Song/Mincho

Gothic

The original meaning of character "食" (to eat): to dine with good appetite.

◉ *Oracle bone script:*
It consists of the signs of a mouth and a footed vessel.

◉ *Seal script:*
The foot of vessel was changed to "匕"(spoon), to stress the use of a spoon.

◉ *Clerical script:*
The shape of "匕" was changed.

◉ *Oracle bone script*

Bronze script

Seal script

Clerical script

Regular Script

Cursive Script

Semi-cursive Script

Imitation Song

Song/Mincho

Gothic

The original meaning of character "宰" (slaughter): slaves slaughtered livestock in a house for sacrifice.

◉ *Oracle bone script:*
It is the combination of "宀" (house) and "辛"(knife).

◉ *Oracle bone script*

Bronze script

Seal script

Clerical script

Regular Script

Cursive Script

Semi-cursive Script

Imitation Song

Song/Mincho

Gothic

The original meaning of character "乐" (music): music.

◉ *Oracle bone script:*
It consists of the shape of two strings and the sign "木" (instrument stand), resembling the shape of a musical instrument.

◉ *Bronze script:*
The sign "白" (to speak and sing) was added in the middle.

▲Simplified Character:
The simplified character "乐" was based on the form in cursive script.

◉ *Oracle bone script*

Bronze script

Seal script

Clerical script

Regular Script

Cursive Script

Semi-cursive Script

Imitation Song

Song/Mincho

Gothic

The original meaning of character "折" (to break):
to cut a tree into two with an axe.

◉ *Oracle bone script:*
It consists of the signs of a broken tree and an axe.

◉ *Bronze script:*
The sign of the axe was changed into "斤".

◉ *Seal script:*
The sign of the broken tree was changed to the sign "手" (hand).

◉ *Clerical script:*
The sign of the hand was simplified into "扌".

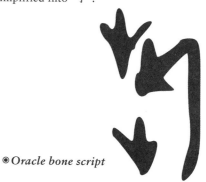
◉ *Oracle bone script*

Bronze script

Seal script

Clerical script

Regular Script

Cursive Script

Semi-cursive Script

Imitation Song

Song/Mincho

Gothic

The original meaning of character "养" (to raise a child):
to shepherd.

◉ *Oracle bone script:*
It consists of the signs of a sheep and a hand waving a whip.

◉ *Seal script:*
It is the combination of "羊"(sheep) and "食" (to feed),
meaning to feed sheep with grass.

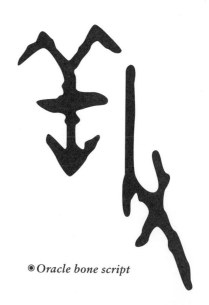
◉ *Oracle bone script*

Bronze script

Seal script

Clerical script

Regular Script

Cursive Script

Semi-cursive Script

Imitation Song

Song/Mincho

Gothic

The original meaning of character "礼" (ceremony):
people worshiped ancestors and gods with good jade and wine.

◉ *Oracle bone script:*
It resembles a sacrificial utensil with two strings of jade.

◉ *Seal script:*
The sign "示" was added.

▲Simplified Character:
In the simplified character "礼",
"豊" was changed into "乙".

◉ *Oracle bone script*

Bronze script

Seal script

Clerical script

Regular Script

Cursive Script

Semi-cursive Script

Imitation Song

Song/Mincho

Gothic

The original meaning of character "好" (good):
giving birth to a child is considered a good thing.

◉ *Oracle bone script:*
It is the combination of the signs "女"(woman) and "子"(child).

◉ *Oracle bone script*

Bronze script

Seal script

Clerical script

Regular Script

Cursive Script

Semi-cursive Script

Imitation Song

Song/Mincho

Gothic

The original meaning of character "弃" (to discard):
a newborn baby is abandoned in a basket

◉*Oracle bone script:*
It consists of the signs "子" (child) and "其" (bamboo basket),
three drops of water (representiing amniotic fluid), and two hands,
which indicates the act of abandoning a child.

◉*Bronze script:*
The sign "子" was turned upside down to signify a newborn baby.

◉*Seal script:*
The shape of "其" was transformed.

◉*Clerical script:*
The shapes of the inverted "子" and
two hands were transformed.

▲Simplified Character:
The simplified character "弃" inherits
from the simplified form in seal script.

◉*Oracle bone script*

Bronze script

Seal script

Clerical script

Regular Script

Cursive Script

Semi-cursive Script

Imitation Song

Song/Mincho

Gothic

The original meaning of character "令" (order):
to give a command.

◉*Oracle bone script:*
It consists of the shapes of a mouth facing down and a
kneeling man, indicating the act of a superior giving
command to a subordinate.

◉*Seal script:*
The shape of the man was simplified.

◉*Oracle bone script*

Bronze script

Seal script

Clerical script

Regular Script

Cursive Script

Semi-cursive Script

Imitation Song

Song/Mincho

Gothic

The original meaning of character "合" (to close):
to lock or to close.

◉ *Oracle bone script:*
It is the combination of the shapes of a lid and a container.

◉ *Clerical script:*
The upper part was transformed into the combination of
"人" and "一".

◉ *Oracle bone script*

Bronze script

Seal script

Clerical script

Regular Script

Cursive Script

Semi-cursive Script

Imitation Song

Song/Mincho

Gothic

The original meaning of character "舞" (dance):
to sing and dance in sacrificial ceremony with flowering branches
in hand.

◉ *Oracle bone script:*
It resembles the shape of a man waving flowering branches.

◉ *Bronze script:*
The signs of hands and flowering branches were separated with
the addition of the "口" (mouth) to each "branch" and the "舛"
(to walk) to the bottom.

◉ *Seal script:*
The sign "辵" (two legs) was added to emphasize
the movement of legs.

◉ *Clerical script:*
The signs of man and hands disappeared.

◉ *Oracle bone script*

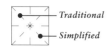

Bronze script

Seal script

Clerical script

Regular Script

Cursive Script

Semi-cursive Script

Imitation Song

Song/Mincho

Gothic

The original meaning of character "送" (to escort):
the bridesmaids accompany the bride and hold umbrellas for her.

◉*Bronze script:*
It consists of five parts: "彳" (to walk), "二" (two men),
"止" (foot), the shape of an umbrella, and the sign of two hands.

◉*Seal script:*
"彳" and "止" were combined into "辵"; the shape of the umbrella
was changed into "火" (fire); the "二" was omitted.

◉*Clerical script:*
The combination of "火" and "two hands" was changed
into "关"; the "辵" was simplified into "辶".

Bronze script

Seal script

Clerical script

Regular Script

Cursive Script

Semi-cursive Script

Imitation Song

Song/Mincho

Gothic

The original meaning of character "习" (to practise):
young birds flap their wings to practise flying in the nest.

◉*Oracle bone script:*
It consists of "羽" (feather) and "口" (resembling the shape of
a nest). In other forms, "日" (sun) was used instead of "口".

◉*Seal script:*
The "日" was changed into "白".

▲*Simplified Character:*
In the simplified character "习",
one "习" was removed from "羽"
and "日" was omitted.

◉*Oracle bone script*

Bronze script

Seal script

Clerical script

Regular Script

Cursive Script

Semi-cursive Script

Imitation Song

Song/Mincho

Gothic

The original meaning of character "献" (to offer):
to cook preys in a tripod to worship gods.

◉ *Oracle bone script:*
It consists of two signs "鬲" (tripod) and "犬" (dog).

◉ *Bronze script:*
The sign "虍" (tiger) was added to signify better offerings to gods.

◉ *Oracle bone script*

Bronze script

Seal script

Clerical script

Regular Script

Cursive Script

Semi-cursive Script

Imitation Song

Song/Mincho

Gothic

The original meaning of character "言" (to speak):
to talk with one's tongue.

◉ *Oracle bone script:*
It is the combination of the shape of a tongue and a short rightward
stroke indicating the act of speaking initiated by a tongue.

◉ *Clerical script:*
The shape of a tongue was simplified into three rightward strokes.

◉ *Oracle bone script*

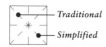
Traditional
Simplified

Bronze script

Seal script

Clerical script

Regular Script

Cursive Script

Semi-cursive Script

Imitation Song

Song/Mincho

Gothic

The original meaning of character "寝" (to sleep):
the emperor slept with his servants fanning for him.

◉ *Oracle bone script:*
It combines the "宀" (the imperial palace)
and the sign of a feather fan.

◉ *Seal script:*
The sign "人" (man) was added.

◉ *Clerical script:*
The "人" was replaced by "爿"(bed) to stress the sleeping on a bed.

In the simplified character "寝",
"爿" was simplified into "丬" according
to Simplification by Analogy.

◉ *Oracle bone script*

Bronze script

Seal script

Clerical script

Regular Script

Cursive Script

Semi-cursive Script

Imitation Song

Song/Mincho

Gothic

The original meaning of character "杀" (to kill):
to slaughter and skin the animals.

◉ *Oracle bone script:*
It combines the signs "又" (to catch) and "毛" (animals' fur).

◉ *Seal script:*
It consists of "又" (to catch), "术" (to skin), and "殳" (to attack with weapons), stressing the act of peeling off animal's fur after slaughter.

▲**Simplified Character:**
In the simplified character "杀", "殳" was omitted.

◉ *Oracle bone script*

Bronze script

Seal script

Clerical script

Regular Script

Cursive Script

Semi-cursive Script

Imitation Song

Song/Mincho

Gothic

The original meaning of character "交" (to intersect): standing with two crossed legs.

◉ *Oracle bone script:*
It resembles a man with his leg crossed.

◉ *Clerical script:*
It became the combination of "六" and "乂" without the shape of "人"(man).

◉ *Oracle bone script*

Bronze script

Seal script

Clerical script

Regular Script

Cursive Script

Semi-cursive Script

Imitation Song

Song/Mincho

Gothic

The original meaning of character "育" (to give birth): a woman gives birth to a child.

◉ *Oracle bone script:*
It consists of the signs "女" (female) and the inverted "子" (infant).

◉ *Bronze script:*
Three dots were added to the "head" of "子" as a sign of the amniotic fluid.

◉ *Seal script:*
It consists of the signs of an infant and "肉" (fresh, meaning to raise).

◉ *Clerical script:*
The sign "肉" was changed into "月".

◉ *Oracle bone script*

Bronze script

Seal script

Clerical script

Regular Script

Cursive Script

Semi-cursive Script

Imitation Song

Song/Mincho

Gothic

The original meaning of character "行" (to walk): a crossroad.

◉ *Oracle bone script:*
It resembles a crossroad.

◉ *Oracle bone script*

Bronze script

Seal script

Clerical script

Regular Script

Cursive Script

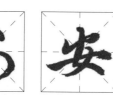

Semi-cursive Script

Imitation Song

Song/Mincho

Gothic

The original meaning of character "安" (peaceful): a woman feels secure living in a house.

◉ *Oracle bone script:*
It combines the signs "宀" (house) and "女" (female).

◉ *Oracle bone script*

Bronze script

Seal script

Clerical script

Regular Script

Cursive Script

Semi-cursive Script

Imitation Song

Song/Mincho

Gothic

The original meaning of character "禽" (fowl):
the original character of "擒" (to catch birds with a net).

◉ *Oracle bone script:*
It consists of the shape of a net and "十" (the handle of a net).

◉ *Bronze script:*
A sign of the lid was added above, meaning to place the birds
in an enclosed space.

◉ *Oracle bone script*

The original meaning of character "射" (to shoot):
to shoot an arrow to a distant target.

◉ *Oracle bone script:*
It demonstrates the act of shooting an arrow from a bow.

◉ *Bronze script:*
The sign of the hand was added to signify the act of
holding the arrow.

◉ *Seal script:*
The "bow" and "arrow" were combined into "身".

Bronze script

Seal script

Clerical script

Regular Script

Cursive Script

Semi-cursive Script

Imitation Song

Song/Mincho

Gothic

◉ *Oracle bone script*

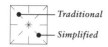
Traditional

Simplified

Bronze script

Seal script

Clerical script

Regular Script

Cursive Script

Semi-cursive Script

Imitation Song

Song/Mincho

Gothic

The original meaning of character "饮" (to drink): to drink.

◉ *Oracle bone script:*
It consists of the signs of the act of holding a wine cup and a tongue (to taste).

◉ *Bronze script:*
The sign of the tongue was changed into mouth, the combination of "人" and "一".

◉ *Clerical script:*
The left part was replaced by "食", and the right part was replaced by "欠".

▲ **Simplified Character:**
The simplified character "饮" is based on the form in cursive script.

◉ *Oracle bone script*

Bronze script

Seal script

Clerical script

Regular Script

Cursive Script

Semi-cursive Script

Imitation Song

Song/Mincho

Gothic

The original meaning of character "孝" (filial piety): supporting and waiting upon parents or the elders.

◉ *Oracle bone script:*
It is the combination of the signs "老" (old) above and "子" (child) below.

◉ *Bronze script:*
The sign "老" was emphasized.

◉ *Clerical script: :*
The sign "老" was simplified and the sign "子" took form.

◉ *Oracle bone script*

Bronze script

Seal script

Clerical script

Regular Script

Cursive Script

Semi-cursive Script

Imitation Song

Song/Mincho

Gothic

The original meaning of character "宿" (to stay overnight):
to sleep on a mat overnight in a house.

◉ *Oracle bone script:*
It is the combination of the signs of a mat,
"人" (man), and "宀" (house).

◉ *Seal script:*
The sign of the mat was changed into "西".

◉ *Oracle bone script*

Bronze script

Seal script

Clerical script

Regular Script

Cursive Script

Semi-cursive Script

Imitation Song

Song/Mincho

Gothic

The original meaning of character "弹" (to catapult):
to shoot small hard balls with bowstrings.

◉ *Oracle bone script:*
It consists of a bow with bowstring and a circle
(a small hard ball).

◉ *Seal script:*
The sign of bow was simplified, and "單" (a weapon made of
twig and stones) was used to replace the sign of ball.

▲**Simplified Character:**
In the simplified character "弹", the two "口" in "單" were
simplified into two dots according to the rules of cursive script.

◉ *Oracle bone script*

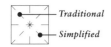

Bronze script

Seal script

Clerical script

Regular Script

Cursive Script

Semi-cursive Script

Imitation Song

Song/Mincho

Gothic

The original meaning of character "穿" (to penetrate):
to punch through.

◉*Bronze script:*
It combines the signs "牙" (molars) and "穴" (cave).

Bronze script

Seal script

Clerical script

Regular Script

Cursive Script

Semi-cursive Script

Imitation Song

Song/Mincho

Gothic

The original meaning of character "盜" (to steal):
to steal other people's utensils out of greediness.

◉*Oracle bone script:*
It consists of two signs "次" (greediness) and "皿" (vessel).

◉*Clerical script:*
The sign of water was changed into two dots "冫".

◉*Oracle bone script*

Bronze script

Seal script

Clerical script

Regular Script

Cursive Script

Semi-cursive Script

Imitation Song

Song/Mincho

Gothic

The original meaning of character "犯" (to violate):
a dog attacks a man.

◉*Bronze script:*
It is the combination of two signs "犬" (dog) and "人" (man).

◉*Clerical script:*
The sign "犬" was simplified into "犭", and "the man being attacked" into "ㄗ".

Bronze script

Seal script

Clerical script

Regular Script

Cursive Script

Semi-cursive Script

Imitation Song

Song/Mincho

Gothic

The original meaning of character "夺" (to snatch):
to scramble for the captured birds.

◉*Bronze script:*
It consists of the signs of a bird flapping its wings
and "又" (to catch).

◉*Clerical script:*
The upper part was changed to "隹" (bird), and the sign "又"
was changed into "寸".

▲**Simplified Character:**
In the simplified character "夺", "隹" was omitted.

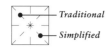

Bronze script

Seal script

Clerical script

Regular Script

Cursive Script

Semi-cursive Script

Imitation Song

Song/Mincho

Gothic

The original meaning of character "包" (bag): the amniotic membrane that wraps the fetus.

◉ *Oracle bone script:*

It is the combination of the signs of a membrane and "子" (child).

◉ *Bronze script:*

It resembles a fetus in a membrane.

◉ *Seal script:*

The sign of the membrane was changed into "勹".

◉ *Clerical script:*

The sign "子" was transformed into "巳".

◉ *Oracle bone script*

Bronze script

Seal script

Clerical script

Regular Script

Cursive Script

Semi-cursive Script

Imitation Song

Song/Mincho

Gothic

The original meaning of character "取" (to fetch): to cut off enemy's ears to show battle achievements.

◉ *Oracle bone script:*

It consists of the signs of ear and "又" (to catch).

◉ *Bronze script:*

The sign of the hand was stressed.

◉ *Oracle bone script*

Bronze script

Seal script

Clerical script

Regular Script

Cursive Script

Semi-cursive Script

Imitation Song

Song/Mincho

Gothic

The original meaning of character "游" (travel):
students holding the flags of their clans on a study tour.
"斿"is the original character.

◉ *Oracle bone script:*
It consists of the signs of a flag and "子" (student).

◉ *Seal script:*
A sign of water was added to indicate that students crossed
rivers during their tours.

◉ *Clerical script:*
The sign of water was changed into "氵"
and the right part into "斿".

◉ *Oracle bone script*

Bronze script

Seal script

Clerical script

Regular Script

Cursive Script

Semi-cursive Script

Imitation Song

Song/Mincho

Gothic

The original meaning of character "井" (well):
a deep hole in the ground for extracting water,
with its sides covered with stones or bricks.

◉ *Oracle bone script:*
It resembles a well by two horizontal and two vertical strokes.

◉ *Seal script:*
A dot was added to the middle of the well to indicate the water inside.

◉ *Clerical script:*
The dot was omitted.

◉ *Oracle bone script*

Bronze script

Seal script

Clerical script

Regular Script

Cursive Script

Semi-cursive Script

Imitation Song

Song/Mincho

Gothic

The original meaning of character "墙" (wall):
to build a barn with earthen walls.

◉ *Oracle bone script:*
It consists of the signs "片" (building plates),
two "禾" (crop) and "啬" (barn with earthen walls).

◉ *Seal script:*
The two "禾" were changed into "麦"(wheat).

◉ *Clerical script:*
The "禾" was replaced by "土".

◉ *Oracle bone script*

Bronze script

Seal script

Clerical script

Regular Script

Cursive Script

Semi-cursive Script

Imitation Song

Song/Mincho

Gothic

The original meaning of character "窗" (window):
an opening in the wall for ventilation and lighting.

◉ *Oracle bone script:*
It resembles a round hole with three short bars.

◉ *Bronze script:*
The shape of the hole was changed to rhombic, the bars to fence,
and character "囱" was formed, the original character of "窗".

◉ *Seal script:*
"穴" (cave) was added above "囱".

◉ *Oracle bone script*

Bronze script

Seal script

Clerical script

Regular Script

Cursive Script

Semi-cursive Script

Imitation Song

Song/Mincho

Gothic

The original meaning of character "玉" (jade):
a string of gems.

◉*Oracle bone script:*
It resembles a string of three pieces of gems.

◉*Bronze script:*
With both ends of the string removed, it became very similar
to the character "王".

◉*Clerical script:*
A dot was added to differentiate it from character "王".

◉*Oracle bone script*

Bronze script

Seal script

Clerical script

Regular Script

Cursive Script

Semi-cursive Script

Imitation Song

Song/Mincho

Gothic

The original meaning of character "衣" (clothes):
a clothes with two sleeves.

◉*Oracle bone script:*
It resembles a clothes with two sleeves.

◉*Clerical script:*
The lines were transformed into strokes.

◉*Oracle bone script*

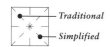

Bronze script

Seal script

Clerical script

Regular Script

Cursive Script

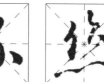
Semi-cursive Script

Imitation Song

Song/Mincho

Gothic

The original meaning of character "丝" (silk): threads drawn from silkworm cocoons.

◉ *Oracle bone script:*
It resembles two strings.

◉ *Bronze script:*
It resembles two strings with knots at one end.

◉ *Clerical script:*
The shape of the end of the string was changed to three dots.

▲ **Simplified Character:**
In the simplified character "丝", the six dots were transformed into a rightward stroke based on the form in cursive script.

◉ *Oracle bone script*

The original meaning of character "巾" (a piece of cloth): accessories made of cloth.

◉ *Oracle bone script:*
It resembles a piece of cloth hung with a strap.

Bronze script

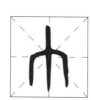
Seal script

Clerical script

Regular Script

Cursive Script

Semi-cursive Script

Imitation Song

Song/Mincho

Gothic

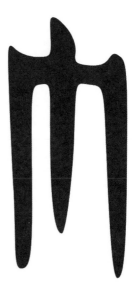
◉ *Oracle bone script*

Bronze script

Seal script

Clerical script

Regular Script

Cursive Script

Semi-cursive Script

Imitation Song

Song/Mincho

Gothic

The original meaning of character "冕" (crown):
ancient officers' hats with tassels.

◉ *Oracle bone script:*
It is the combination of the signs of a hat and a kneeling man,
thus constituting character "免", the original character of "冕".

◉ *Seal script:*
"冃" (hat) was added to the top, and completed the form of "冕".

◉ *Oracle bone script*

Bronze script

Seal script

Clerical script

Regular Script

Cursive Script

Semi-cursive Script

Imitation Song

Song/Mincho

Gothic

The original meaning of character "刀" (knife):
a cutting tool with a sharp edge.

◉ *Oracle bone script:*
It resembles a weapon with a sharp edge and long handle.

◉ *Seal script:*
The shape of the long handle was turned curved.

◉ *Clerical script:*
The shape of the handle disappeared.

◉ *Oracle bone script*

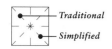

Bronze script

Seal script

Clerical script

Regular Script

Cursive Script

Semi-cursive Script

Imitation Song

Song/Mincho

Gothic

The original meaning of character "网" (net):
a fishing equipment woven with ropes.

◉*Oracle bone script:*
It resembles the shape of a net stretching
between two stakes.

◉*Clerical script:*
The "糸" (string) was added to emphasize
that nets are woven with strings.

▲Simplified Character:
The simplified character "网" was
based on the form in seal script.

◉*Oracle bone script*

Bronze script

Seal script

Clerical script

Regular Script

Cursive Script

Semi-cursive Script

Imitation Song

Song/Mincho

Gothic

The original meaning of character "皿" (vessel):
a type of uncovered goblet.

◉*Oracle bone script:*
It resembles an uncovered goblet with ears.

◉*Seal script:*
The two ears were represented by two
downward strokes instead.

◉*Clerical script:*
The upper part was omitted and the lower part
was transformed into "皿".

◉*Oracle bone script*

Bronze script

Seal script

Clerical script

Regular Script

Cursive Script

Semi-cursive Script

Imitation Song

Song/Mincho

Gothic

The original meaning of character "斗" (ladle):
"spoon" (斗) and "to fight" (鬥).

⦾ **Oracle bone script:**
"斗" resembles a deep spoon with a handle. "鬥" resembles the
scenario of the fight between two men.

⦾ **Bronze script:**
"斗" was slightly changed from the form in oracle bone script.

⦾ **Seal script:**
For "斗", the shape of a spoon faded and it was formed by
strokes. For "鬥", the two men composing the character were
separated with space in between.

⦾ **Clerical script:**
For "鬥", in order to
distinguish from "門"(door),
"豆" and "寸" were added inside.

⦾ Oracle bone script

Bronze script

Seal script

Clerical script

Regular Script

Cursive Script

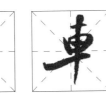
Semi-cursive Script

Imitation Song

Song/Mincho

Gothic

The original meaning of character "车" (cart):
battle vehicles with wheels driven by cattle and horses.

⦾ **Oracle bone script:**
It resembles a vehicle with wheels on both sides driven by animals.

⦾ **Bronze script:**
The sign of a yoke was added.

⦾ **Seal script:**
The sign of two wheels were changed to one.

▲**Simplified Character:**
The simplified character "车" was based on the
form in cursive script.

⦾ Oracle bone script

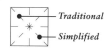

Bronze script

Seal script

Clerical script

Regular Script

Cursive Script

Semi-cursive Script

Imitation Song

Song/Mincho

Gothic

The original meaning of character "舟" (boat):
wooden boats used to cross rivers.

◉*Oracle bone script:*
It resembles a wooden boat, with a ship's rail, bow and stern.

◉*Oracle bone script*

Bronze script

Seal script

Clerical script

Regular Script

Cursive Script

Semi-cursive Script

Imitation Song

Song/Mincho

Gothic

The original meaning of character "东" (east):
a bag wrapped by cloth and wooden sticks carried by travelers.

◉*Oracle bone script:*
It resembles a bag fastened with straps.

▲**Simplified Character:**
The simplified character "东" is based on the form in cursive script.

◉*Oracle bone script*

Bronze script

Seal script

Clerical script

Regular Script

Cursive Script

Semi-cursive Script

Imitation Song

Song/Mincho

Gothic

The original meaning of character "西" (west): baggages used by women in ancient China.

◉ *Oracle bone script:*
It resembles a baggage wound around with ropes.

◉ *Bronze script:*
A sign of a handle was added above.

◉ *Seal script:*
The shape of the handle was transformed.

◉ *Clerical script:*
The shapes of the handle and baggage were changed.

◉ *Oracle bone script*

Bronze script

Seal script

Clerical script

Regular Script

Cursive Script

Semi-cursive Script

Imitation Song

Song/Mincho

Gothic

The original meaning of character "兄" (elder brother): the original character of "祝" (to pray), the elders pray in rituals in ancient times.

◉ *Oracle bone script:*
It is the combination of "口" (mouth) and "人" (man).

◉ *Clerical script:*
The lower part was simplified into "儿".

◉ *Oracle bone script*

Projects
Based on Hanzi

Chinese oracle bone inscriptions (ancient Chinese characters carved on tortoise shells or animal bones) are originally pictorial records that depict objects. The designer re-created a series of ancient Chinese characters to present their intriguing origins and bring them closer to modern graphic design world.

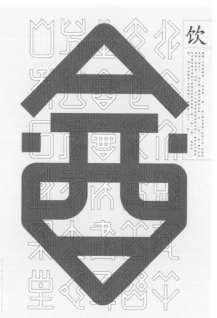

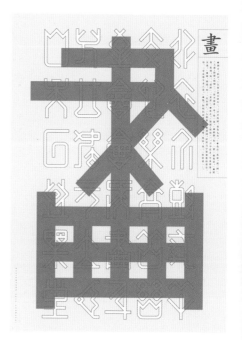

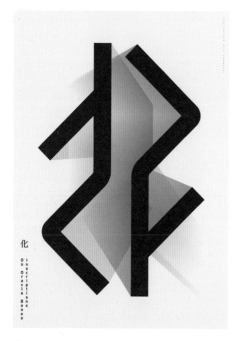

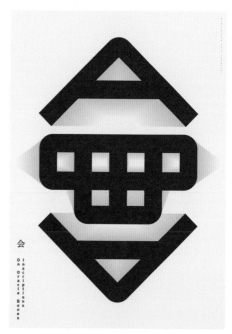

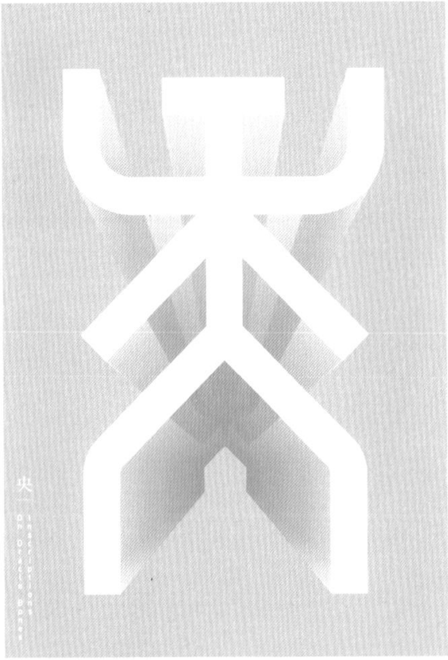

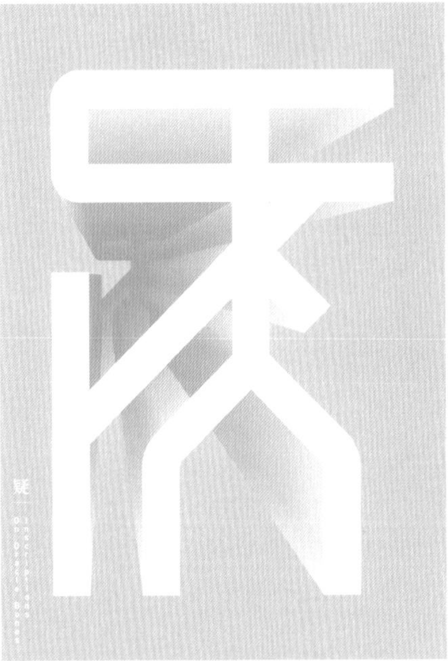

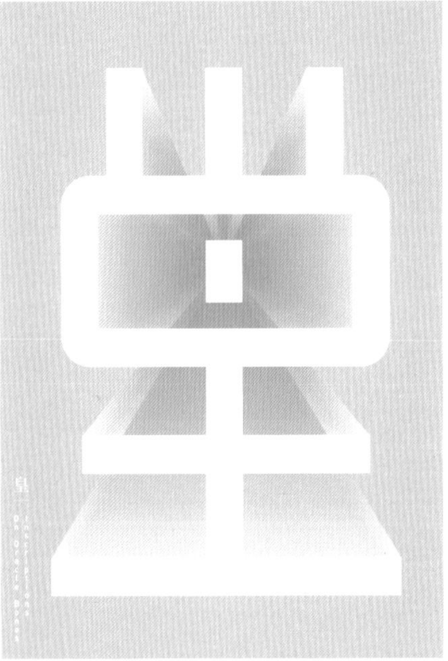

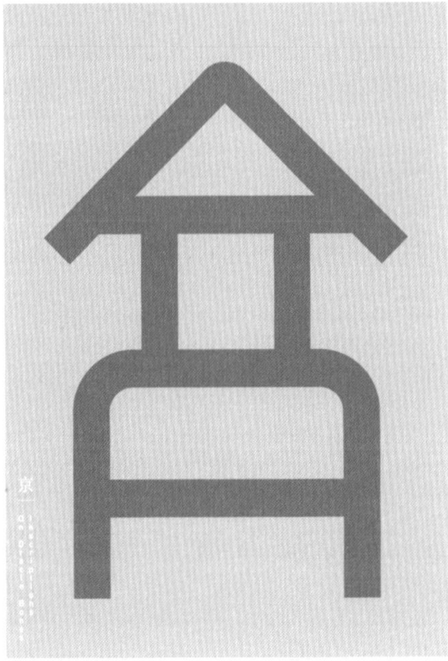

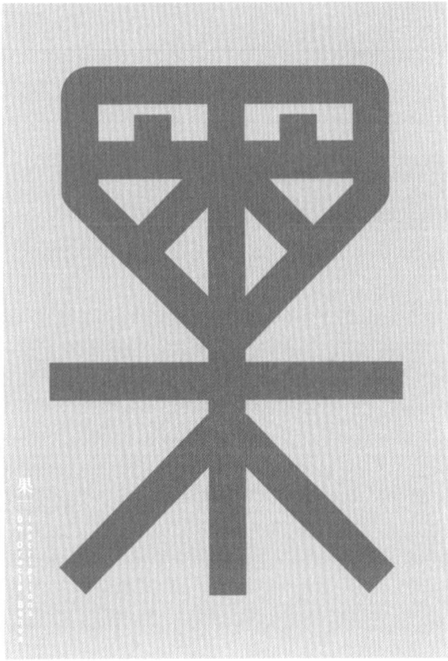

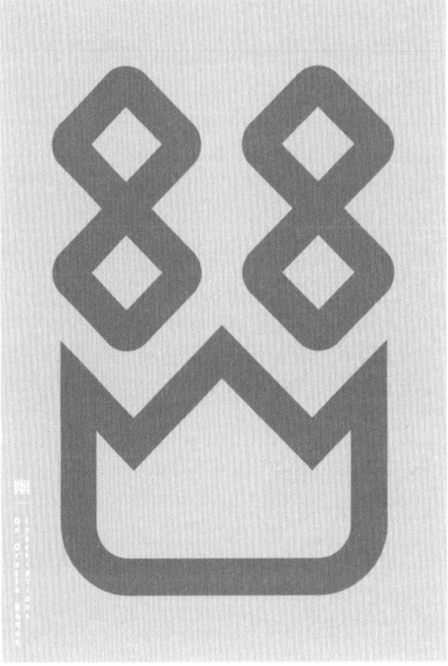

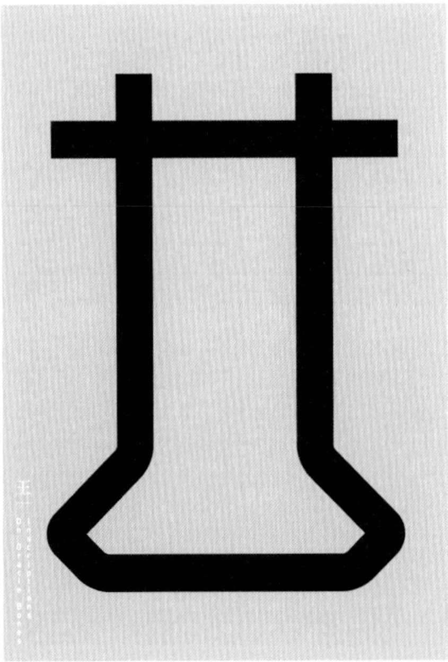

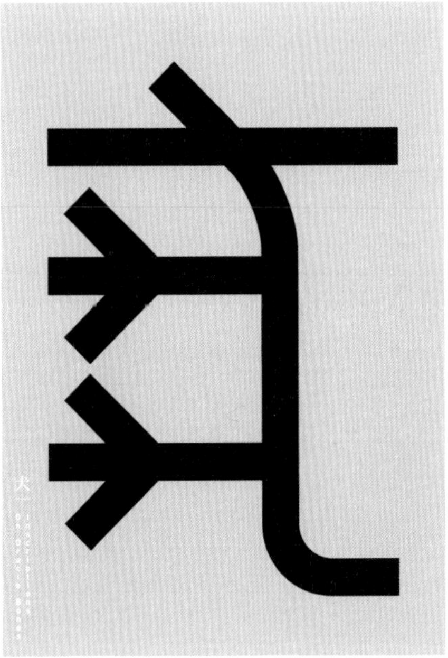

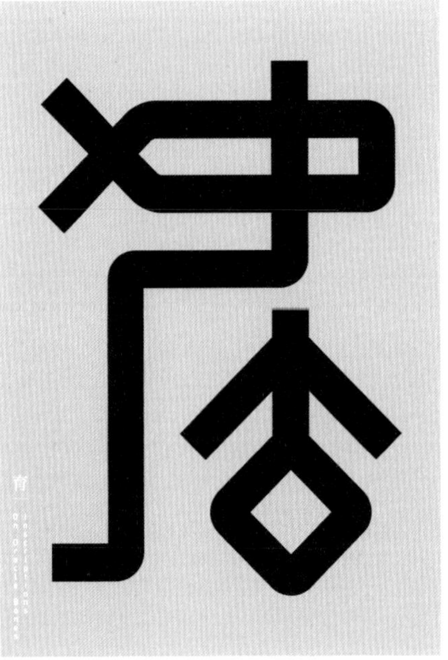

Inscriptions
On Oracle Bones

Inscriptions
On Oracle Bones

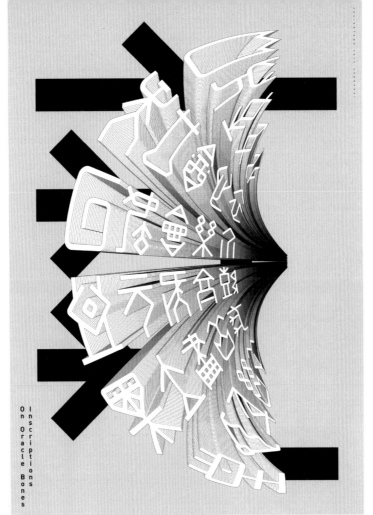

The 12 animal zodiac signs are important cultural symbols in China and the rest of Asia when people talk about calendar and the change of years. It is quite common that New Year's Card would take the 12 animal zodiac signs as a main theme. The Art Décor style that the Studio-Takeuma employs demonstrates a blend of comic streaks that reminds viewers of their memory of reading children's book about the 12 animals in the zodiac system.

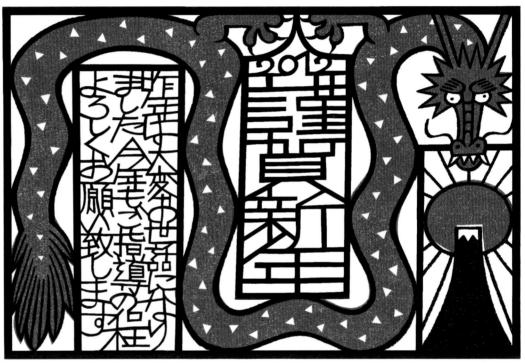

Ethnodrama

Design: **Benny Leung**
Design Agency: **STUDIO-M**
Client: **Centre for Community Cultural Development**

Ethnodrama is a people-oriented drama education program using three different theatrical techniques to put on three performances. In the main visual, the elements of facial expressions and body movements were applied in the logotype design, adding a more dramatic effect to the project.

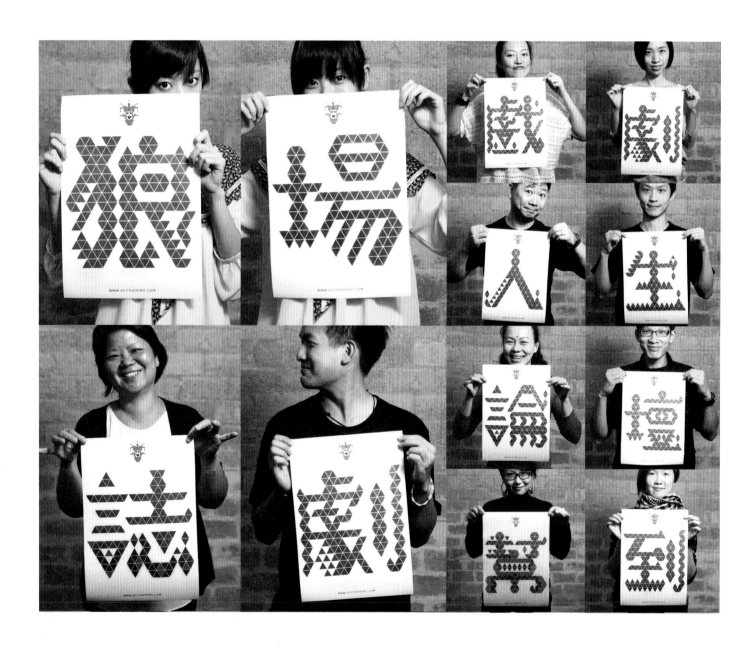

ETHNODRAMA,
LIVING THEATRE &
FORUM THEATRE
SERIES 1,2,3

人種誌
戲劇
生活劇場
論壇劇場
系列
1/2/3

ACT MY LIFE
1/玩▲演▲完

CAN HELP, CAN HELP?!
2/幫到▲幫到?!

SHEEP WITH THE SKIN OF WOLVES
3/披著狼皮的羊

WOLF

FORUM

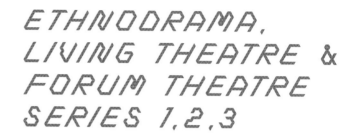

ETHNODRAMA,
LIVING THEATRE &
FORUM THEATRE
SERIES 1,2,3

SHEEP

HELP

ETHNODRAMA,
LIVING THEATRE &
FORUM THEATRE
SERIES 1,2,3

DRAMA

IDEAL

ETHNODRAMA,
LIVING THEATRE &
FORUM THEATRE
SERIES 1,2,3

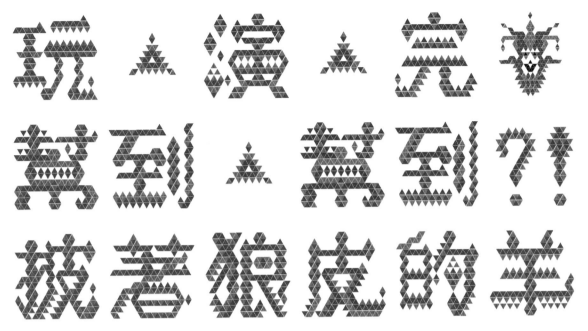

Hanzi (or Kanji) culture is most popular in China and Japan. Strokes, such as horizontal stroke, vertical strokes, and dot, are the foundation of Hanzi. The basic way to show Hanzi is through calligraphy, and the beauty of calligraphy lies in the elegant curves of the strokes.

STROKES OF A CHINESE CHARACTER

THE ART OF CHINESE (KANJI) CALLIGRPAHY

筆畫 / 文字基礎

世界
漢字

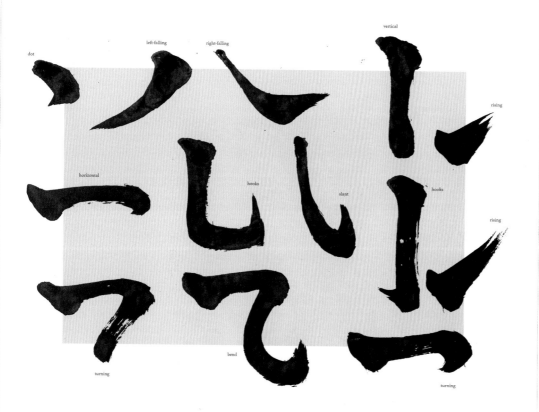

CHINA （中國） / JAPAN （日本）

TOP **2** COUNTRY
WITH KANJI CULTURE
IN THE WORLD

CHARACTER CULTURE
AND HISTORY

awt design Inc.

CREATIVE DIRECTOR: LOK NG
CALLIGRAPHER: LOK NG
PHOTOGRAPHER: TOMI TANG

Sunhwa Arts High School
38th Exhibition

Design: *Baek Serah, Park Ki-young*
Art Direction: *Choi Jongwon*
Design Agency: *Chuigraf*
Client: *Sunhwa Arts High School*

The theme of the 38th exhibition of Sunhwa Arts High School was "生, 日常", which in English means "Life, Everyday Life". Since the students had made divers images that reflected some part of their everyday lives, the designers believed the poster image should represent various parts or segments of life. The three Chinese characters were broken into many pieces with holo-graphic hot stamping foil applied on each stroke. These holographic segments change their colors and brightness in different angles, each of which represents various interpretation of "life, everyday life".

"Shan Fei Shan"
Oil Painting Exhibition
Visual Design

Design: *Jill Chang*
Client: *Ovition Art Space*

The poster design was based on a landscape painting. The designer fully utilized the vertically symmetrical Chinese characters "山非山" to present a combination of virtual and real image—half of them are above the water, half appear as shadows in the water, which creates space tension to the characters. The same logotype was applied to the invitation, allowing the visuals to appear as hollowed-out lines to form the images of a landscape painting.

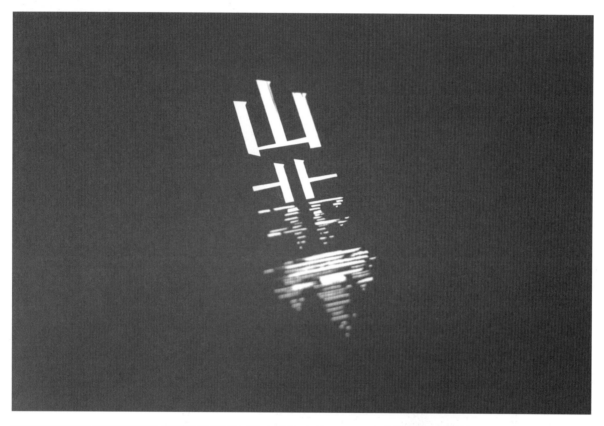

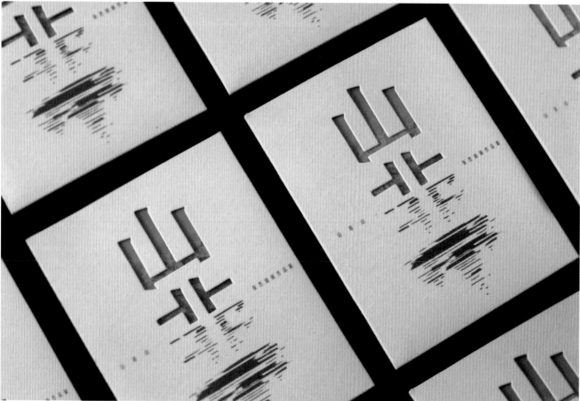

VIP预展
2013.12.14
开幕时间
2013.12.14
展览周期
2013.12.14-2014.02.15
沙龙时间
2013.12.14 15:00-17:00

山 非 山

VIP TIME
2013/12/14
STARTINGTIME
2013/12/14
DURATION
2013/12/14-2014/02/15
SALON TIME
2013.12.14 15:00-17:00

主办单位
北京新绎爱特艺术发展有限公司
主办场地
新绎空间
地 址
北京市朝阳区酒仙桥路2号798艺术区
东街11号高台阶厂库D08
电 话
010-57626258
邮 箱
xinyiart@vip.163.com

张杰油画作品展

SPONSOR
Ovation Art Debelopment Co., Ltd.
LOCATION
Ovation Art Space
ADDRESS
D08 Warehouse, 11 East Street,
798 Art District, 2 Jiuxiangiao
Road,Chaoyang District, Beijing
TELEPHONE
010-57626258
E-MAIL
xinyiart@vip.163.com

SEE YOU
Second-hand Libraire

Design: *Kuhnrae Wu*

SEE YOU ("再見" in Chinese) is a second-hand bookstore.
The designer took half of the two characters "再" and
"見" away, symbolising that people's life is incomplete with
their growing distance with relatives, friends and books.
The bookstore brings people together and encourages them
to meet people who they care about. SEE YOU is not saying
goodbye but a wish to meet again.

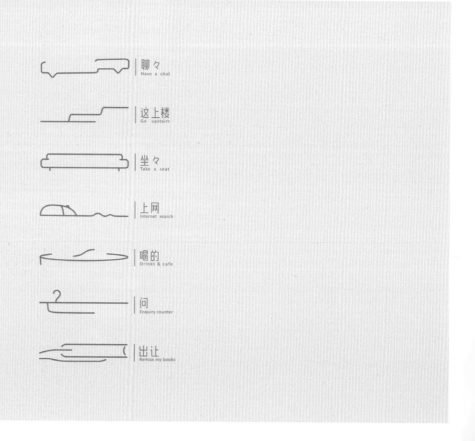

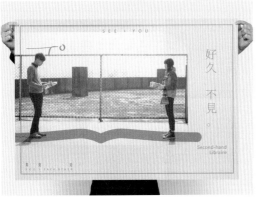

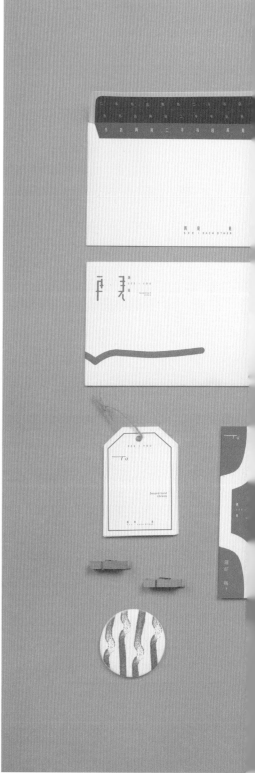

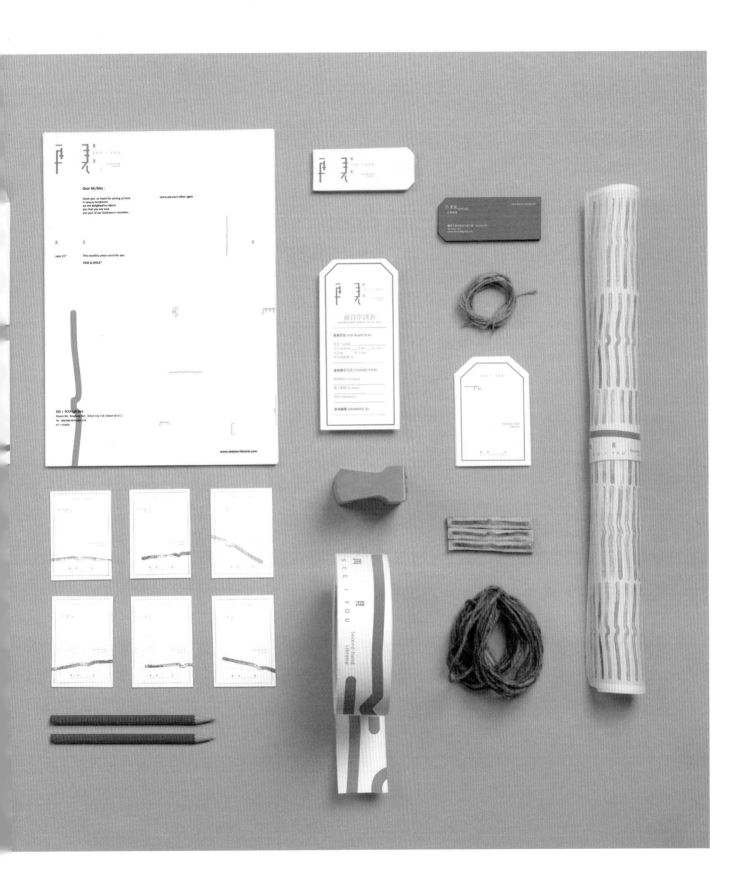

The main products of "Qing He Wu" are tea, chinaware, cloth and images. The brand image combines different design elements including lotus, tea set, etc., presenting a flexible design and eastern Zen-style.

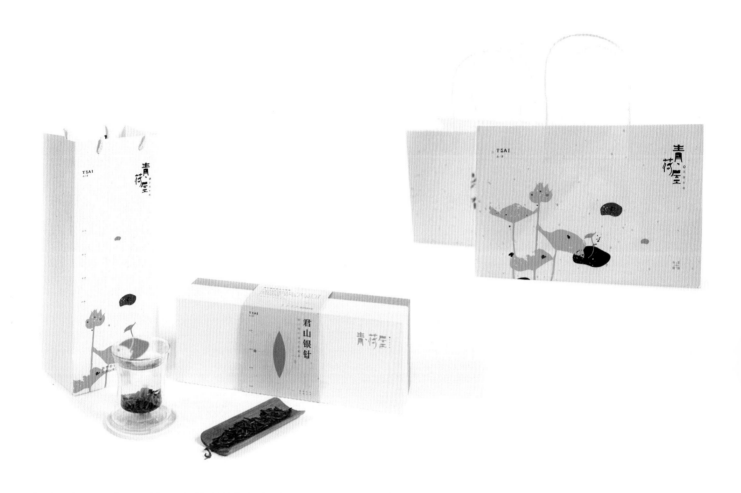

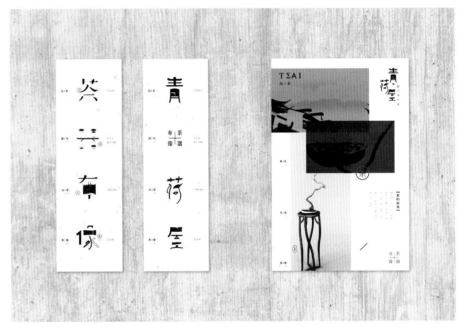

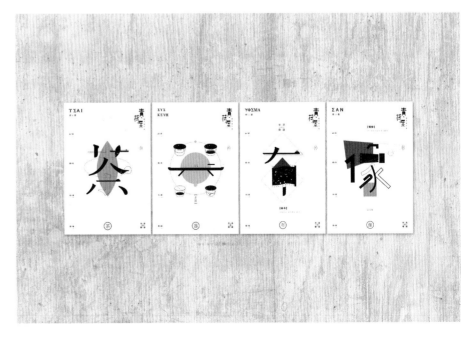

Chinese Skateboard

Design: *Zhan Wei*

This branding was developed for the "Black Knight" project of China Challenge Skateboard Company. Combined with the illustrations in traditional medicine packaging, the lines on the skateboards were inspired by some social issues. The use of variant forms and puns helps to create something playful yet meaningful.

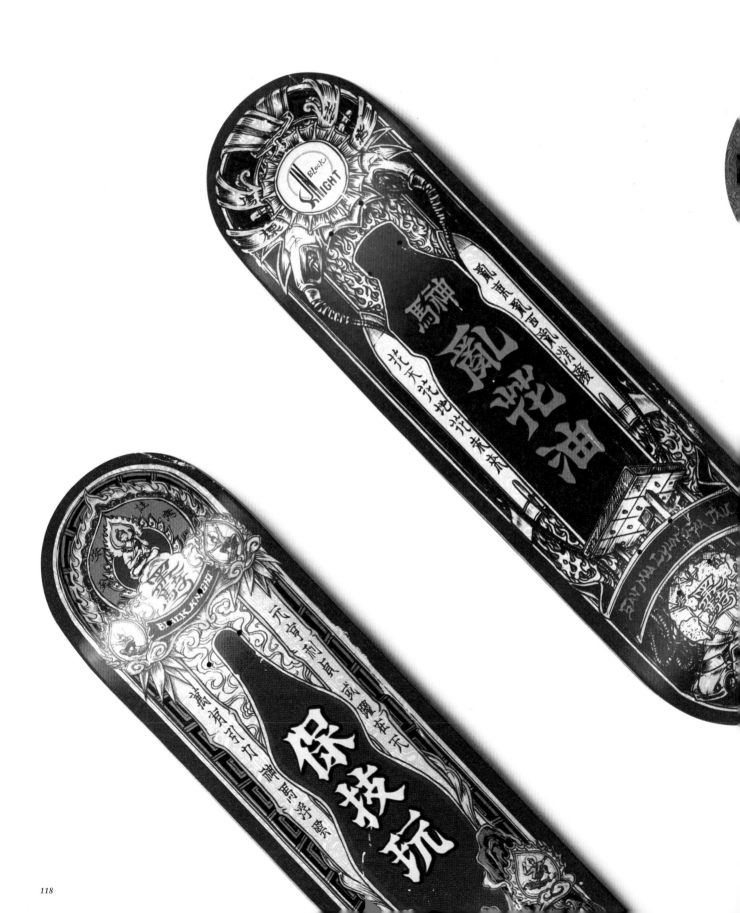

Reiterative Chinese Character Design

Design: *Julio Huang*

The reiterative Chinese character postcard design aims to promote the beauty and wisdom of Chinese characters. All the selected characters are ancient characters used as symbols of auspiciousness. The visual design of every postcard is based on the character's meaning. Friends and families can guess the characters' pronunciations and meanings together as a game while appreciating the beautiful art of Chinese typography.

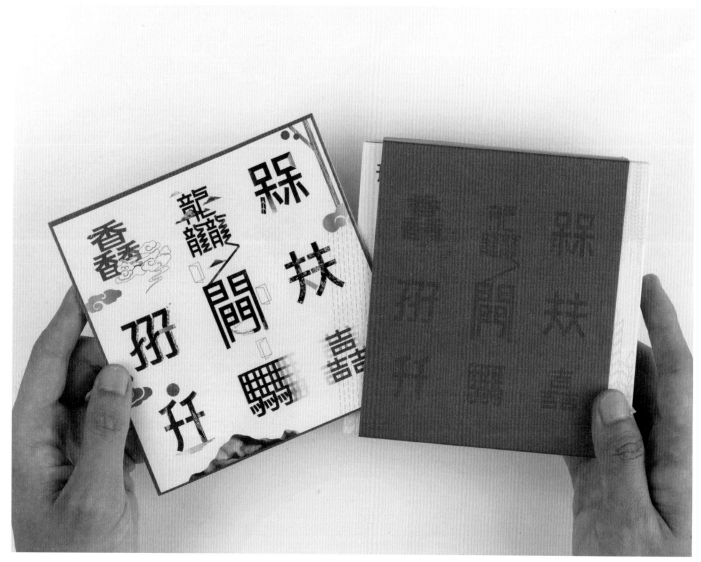

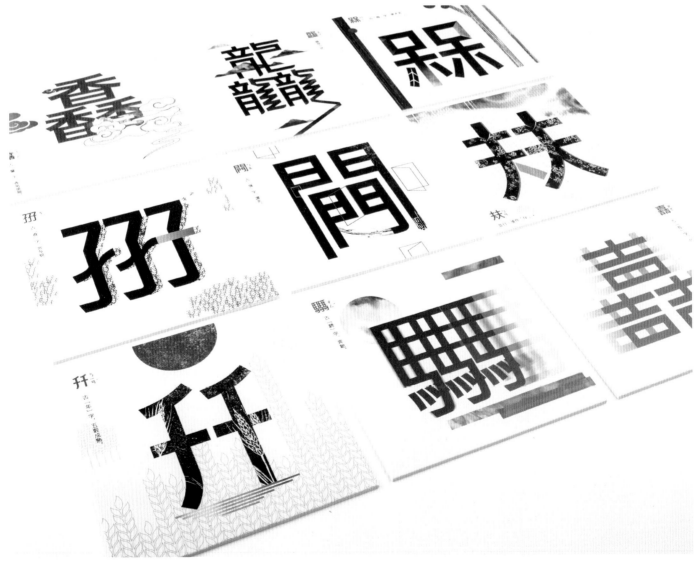

A Life Alive

Design: *Kuhnrae Wu*

"A Life Alive" is the concept of the campaign that aimed to share the festive joy with homeless people during the Chinese Lunar New Year. The campaign supported by donations tried to reverse the public image of the homeless people as "filthy" or "unruly". Everyday utensils such as toothbrushes, toothpaste, and towels all bear the design concept "A Life Alive" to highlight humanity, warmth, and intimacy. They are no longer scary dark figures on the street at night but people who need love like we do.

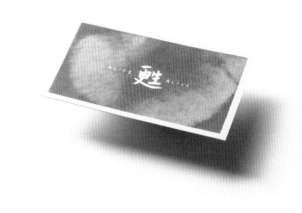

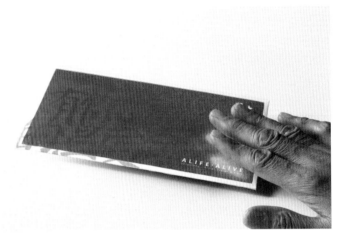

The project was inspired by a warm and sweet memory in the designer's mind where his mother sewed a shirt for him during his childhood. First, she drew the edition type on cloth by a piece of chalk. After tailoring and sewing the cloth, a square cloth was magically transformed into a shirt... Based on the memory, the designer decided to cut the shapes of the strokes that compose the Chinese character "麻" (ramie) out of a piece of ramie cloth, and then recombine the "strokes" to produce a brand new look of the character "麻".

天地之源

縱橫之美

廣源麻品

En Vain Baijiu
Bar & Restaurant

Design: Jacopo Saleri, Gao Yang, Anfia Lin
Creative Direction: Lin Wei, Tang Junhao
Design Agency: United Design Practice
Client: En Vain Baijiu Bar & Restaurant, Li Ke

En Vain (French for "in vain", translated as "白搭" in Chinese) is a Chinese Baijiu (a strong distilled spirit) bar and restaurant for the hip, young and fashionable. Baijiu is perceived to be for an older demographic and old fashioned. The design team has taken the opportunity to reinvent the category, in terms of how Chinese cultural elements can be interpreted in a fresh manner, yet respectful of its historical context. The name En Vain is a direct reference to this playful interpretation of the culture from food and drinks to design.

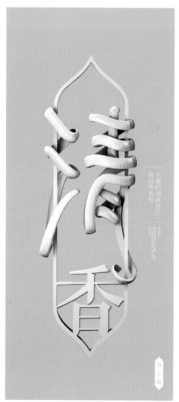

St.James

Design: *YAO & SUSU*
Design Agency: *1983ASIA*

An identity for St.James based on the theme of ceremonial culture. After a research on the typical example of ceremonial culture— Chinese "junzi" and western "gentleman", the designer created a bespoke logotype together with the images of eastern and western "gentleman". Also an Art Deco style was boldly applied to represent a gentle social and cultural cohesion. The logotype is enriched with a series of patterns in magnificent colors.

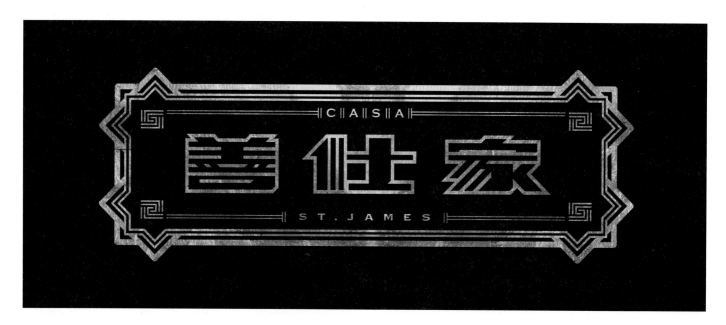

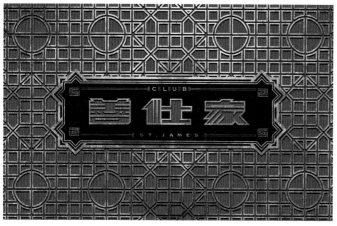

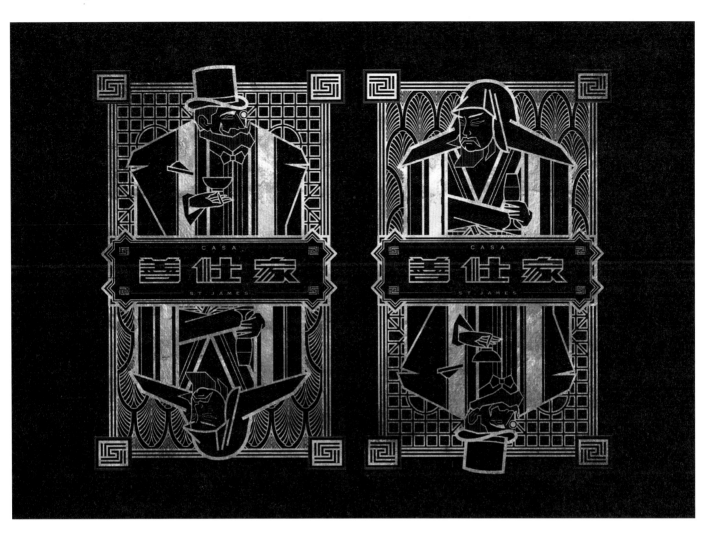

Ginger

Studio: *C&S Brand*
Client: *Ginger Group*

"Ginger" is a new Cantonese restaurant. The designers created a personality for the brand: a yuppie who is manful, stable but natural, self-disciplined but free. They captured the visual images from the character and selected "Kylin" as the core symbol of the brand. The English brand name was written in traditional Chinese calligraphy.

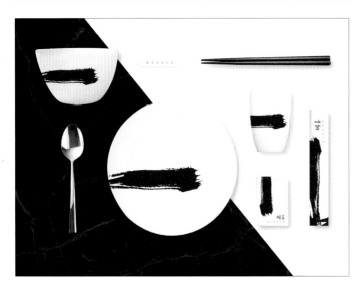

Love for Longyuan

Design Agency: Shenzhen Excel Package Design, Co. Ltd

"陇"(pronounced long) is an alternative name for China's Gansu Province. Designers created a new logotype for this package to represent the characteristic of this area. The main identity of this brand, in the form of paper-cut, shows the life and customs of the people living in this area. The simple white surfaces distinguish themselves on the shelf, while the small transparent "window" allow customers a preview of the content.

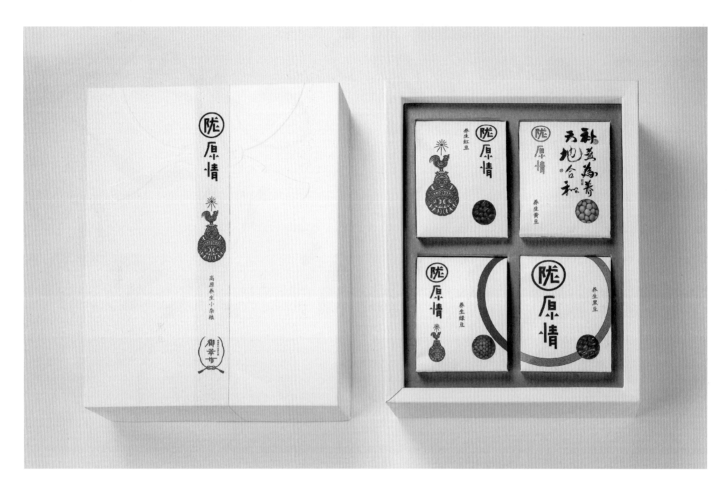

Established in 1965, Sei Kee Cafe "世記咖啡" is widely known for its clay pot brewed coffee and milk tea made in traditional charcoal stove, based on the café's secret recipe. Its Taipa store features in a nostalgic style with a handwritten artistic logo and vintage decoration, recreating a café in the 20th century.

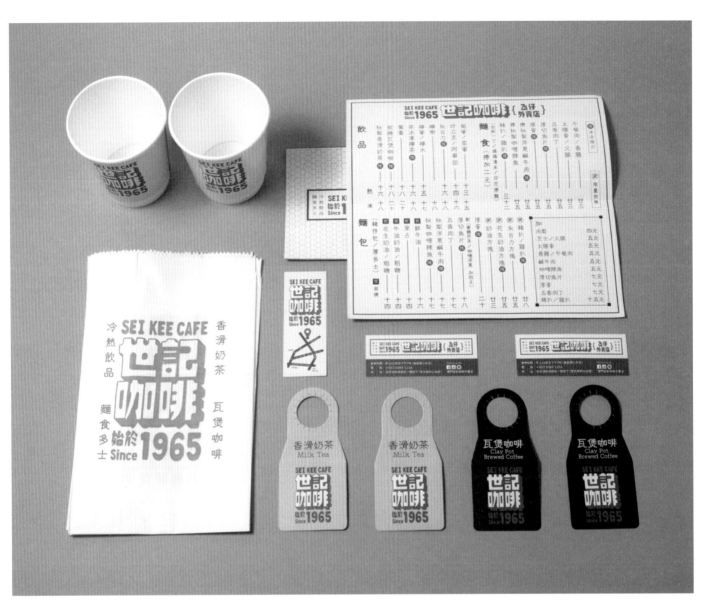

"ShiroPON" "KuroPON"

Design: **Michitomo Sekiura**
Design Agency: **sekiura design**
Creative Director: **Ruriko Sekiura**

The food packaging design was for gourmet MARUSHO. The designer took Kanji as the main element, featuring the calligraphy writing style to present a charm of traditional culture.

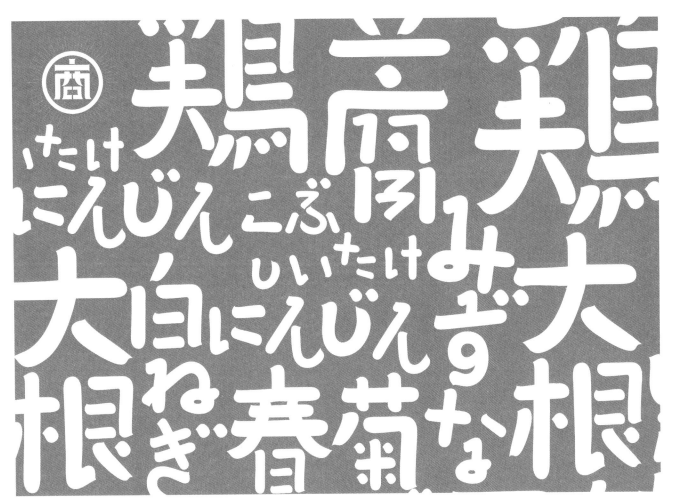

MARUSHO

【HIRA-KANA】　　　　　　　　　　　　　　　【ELEMENTS】

あ　う　わ　い
さ　ゐ　か　ろ
き　の　よ　は
ゆ　お　た　に
め　く　れ　ほ
み　や　そ　へ
し　ま　つ　と
ゑ　け　ね　ち
ひ　ふ　な　り
も　こ　ら　ぬ
せ　え　む　る
す　て　　　を

一　ノ　ヽ
L　つ　ノ
十　の　＼
ノ　1　v
ノ　○　ヽ

SHIRO-pon
525ml

KURO-pon
525ml

139

Tsui Hang Village 40th Anniversary Campaign

Design: Alex Lau, Angel Tsang, Rex Liao
Design Agency: Miramar Group

In celebration of the renowned Cantonese restaurant Tsui Hang Village's 40th birthday, a promotional campaign with a nostalgic feel was created to take foodies on a trip down the memory lane. From the logo to the gift voucher to the dim sum menu, the campaign oozes retro-flair without losing its modern touch. Oil painting, a drawing style wildly popular with cinema advertising back in the 70s, features in the advertisement with house specialty honey-glazed barbecued pork, further evoking Hong Kong's good old days.

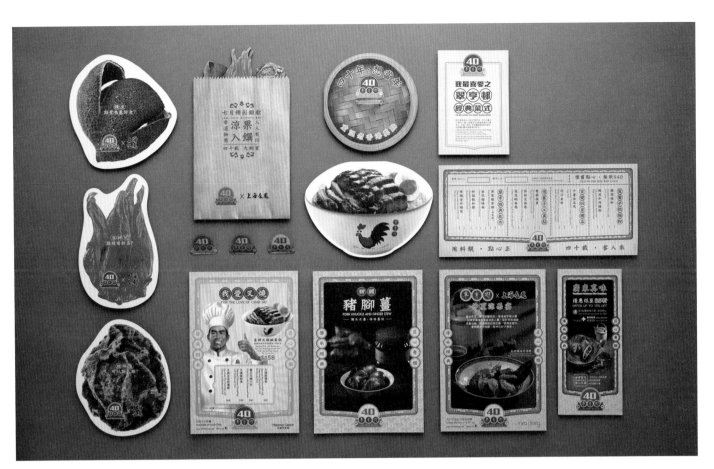

Typephoon—
Exhibition Identity Design

Design: Andrew Wong, Julie Yeh, Karen Tsai,
Charly Chen, Kuan Yu Chen, Fong Ming Yang, Janett Wang
Design Agency: Onion Design Associates
Client: Tien Tien Circle Creative

This is the identity designed for the typographic installation exhibition themed "Typephoon 字" ("字" means character). The exhibition included a series of guest typographical art, cartoons, installation art, alphabetical meals, workshops, documentaries, and talks. The term Typephoon is adapted from "typhoon", the tropical storm from Asia-Pacific area, which is composed of the root "typ-" meaning form and suggests that its power can be as strong as a typhoon. The design team reconstructed "字" with different design elements, overlapping it with the letters of its English title "Typephoon" scattered around as if it were blown away by a typhoon.

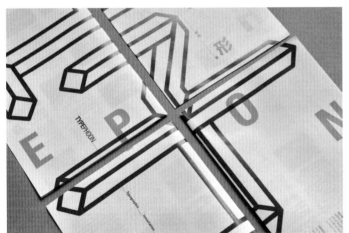

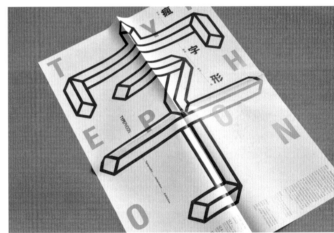

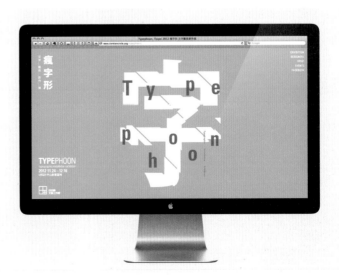

Little Movements— Self-practice in Contemporary Art

Design: *Gu Lei*
Design Agency: *G_Lab_TINYworkshop*
Client: *Shenzhen OCT Contemporary Art Center*

This is an exhibition exploring new methods in artistic and practical researches. The identity of this exhibition features Hanzi as the main design, expressing an idealistic view on literature and art creation through type design. A4 paper is used as a medium to connect texts and paper material.

小运动 当代艺术中的自我实践

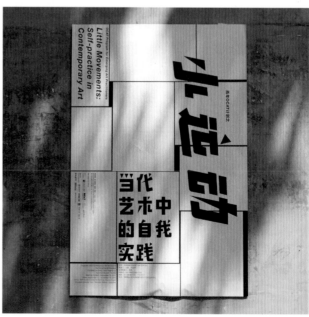

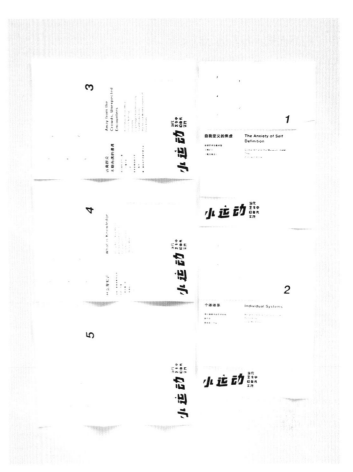

FUN羊—NEW YEAR 2015

Design: **Ken-tsai Lee**
Studio: **SUMP DESIGN**
Design: **Zhuai Chen**
Client: **DD2**

The designers aimed to present a more interesting side of traditional Chinese culture. Classic images on Spring Festival couplets such as Door God, Money God, etc. were blended in the design of the animal "Ram". The designers adopted the geometric shapes to visualize the strokes in Chinese characters.

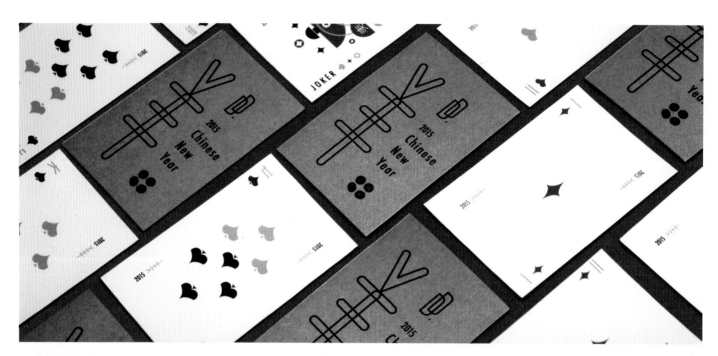

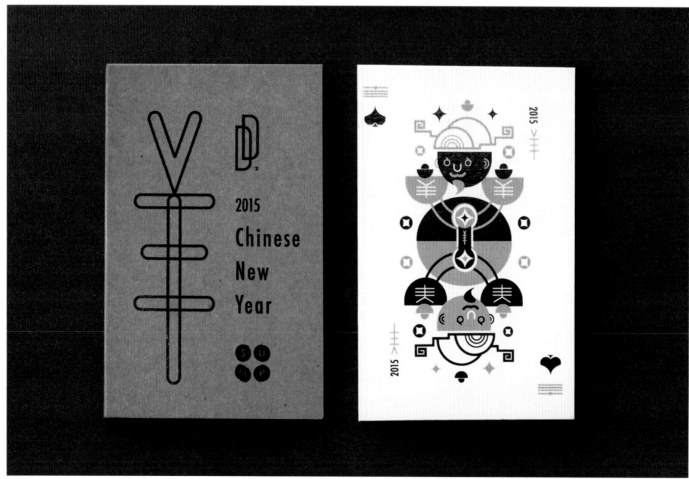

Relationship

Design: *Lok Ng*
Design Agency: *awt design Inc*

Fascinated by the inspirations and ideas from art, the designer has always been trying to blend art and commercial designs, and to create added-value in artworks. In this project Relationship, he has created the calligraphy type designs: flower/love (花/愛), day/month (日/月), and wind/cloud (風/雲).

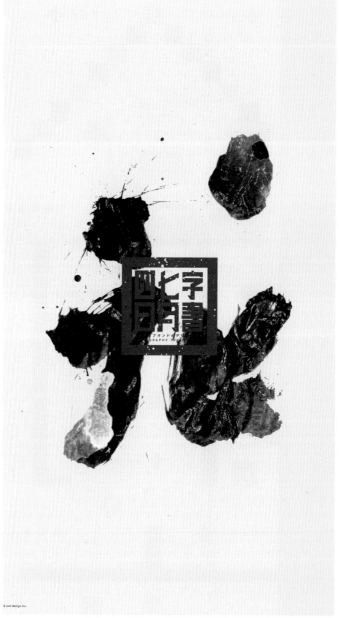

CALLIGRAPHY
TYPE DESIGN

花／愛

LOVE and FLOWER

creative & calligraphy:
Lok Ng

Photography:
Ayu auyeung

@awt design Inc.

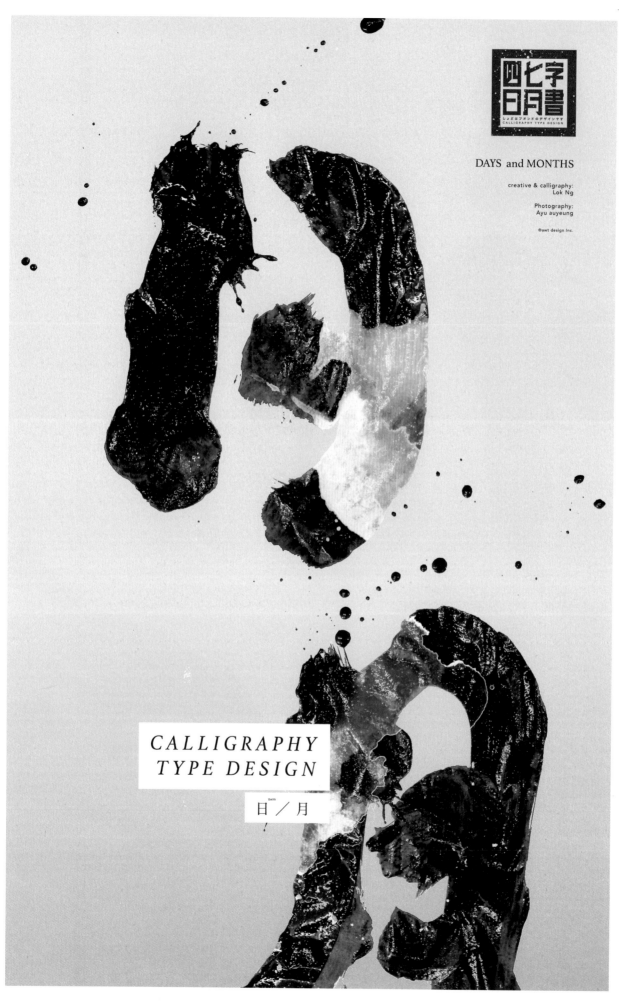

四七字
日月書
しょどはフオンドのデザインです
CALLIGRAPHY TYPE DESIGN

DAYS and MONTHS

creative & calligraphy:
Lok Ng

Photography:
Ayu auyeung

®awt design inc.

CALLIGRAPHY
TYPE DESIGN

日／月

CALLIGRAPHY
TYPE DESIGN

風 ／ 雲
WIND   CLOUD

WIND and CLOUD

creative & calligraphy:
Lok Ng

Photography:
Ayu auyeung

©awt design Inc.

Macau Stories 3—City Mazed

Design: *Li Haoqiang, Zhao Guojun*
Design Agency: *TODOT DESIGN*
Client: *Associação Audio-Visual CUT*

The mirror image of a human head and a skyline of the city alluded to people's lives in Macau, were arranged tactfully to present a film exploring human nature. The characters stand out in bold calligraphy style offering an enhanced visual effect while highlighting the theme of the film.

疑城

City Mazed

堂口
故事
MACAU
STORIES
3

疑城 City Mazed

堂口故事 3
MACAU STORIES

集結澳門本土力量，
3段懸疑故事年底大舉進擊！

Attacking the Titans,
three suspense stories show
their muscles later this year.

Beware!

Coming soon!
www.facebook.com/MS3CityMazed

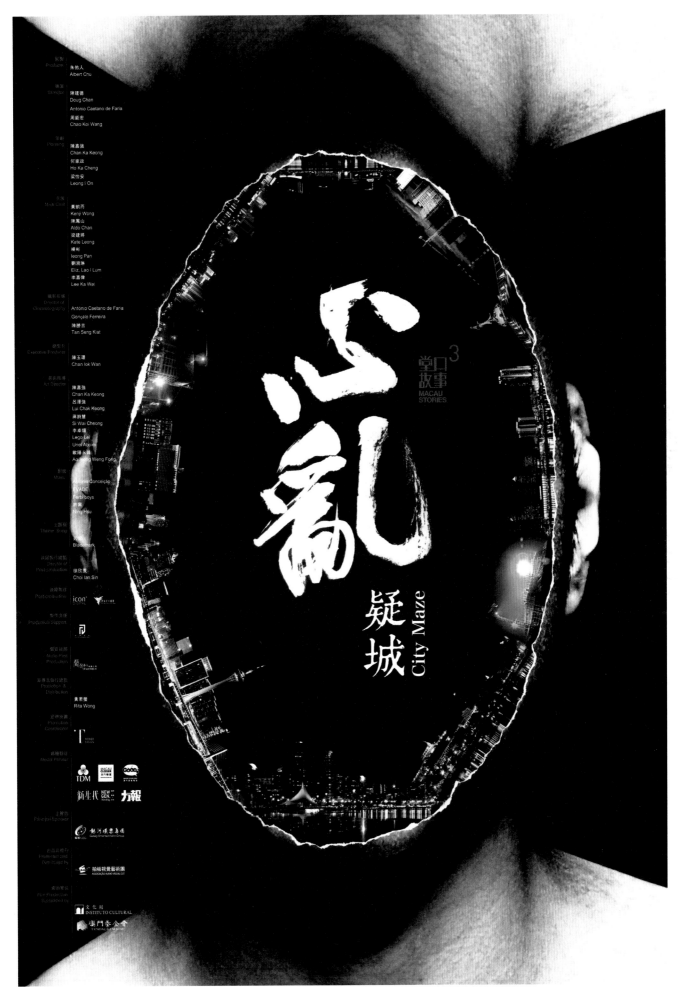

Matsuyama Brand Identity

Design: *Wen Li*
Design Agency: *One&One Design*

Matsuyama is a Japanese restaurant located in the suburban area of Paris, France. For Europeans, Chinese calligraphic elements in the design of the brand can easily remind them of Asia. The black-and-white minimalistic while elegant proportion of the Chinese characters deliver a message of oriental wisdom in terms of health-maintenance and arts of cuisine.

Matsuyama
Restaurant Japonais

La cuisine japonaise,
on n'est pas chose
qui se mange,

mais chose
qui se regarde ...
qui se regarde,

et mieux encore,
qui se médite!

Junichiro Tanizaki

Matsuyama
Restaurant Japonais

La cuisine japonaise,
on n'est pas chose
qui se mange,

mais chose
qui se regarde ...
qui se regarde,

et mieux encore,
qui se médite!

Junichiro Tanizaki

There are two sides to everything, ups ("順", pronounced shun) and downs ("逆", pronounced ni). The greatest time in life is not the moment when you fulfill your dream but when you press on and move forward. Thus, it is worth cherishing the moments of all the ups and downs. Lay down the heavy burdens, leave behind the depressions, and there will be a broader sky to soar.

SHUN / NI

There are two sides to every-thing

Date:
DEC.18.2014
12 18

Creative Director:
Lok Ng

Calligraphy:
Lok Ng

Photography:
Chuck Tang

The greatest thing in life is not the moment when you fulfill your dream, is the times pressing on and moving forward, thus in times of the journey, is worth cherishing the moments of all the ups and downs, nothing needs to change, lay down the heavy burdens, leave behind the depressions, and there will be a broader sky to soar.

Having always been passionate about calligraphy type, the designer observes Chinese characters from different angles and uses the most basic calligraphy to reveal their artistic forms. The ink has brought out the natural texture of Hanzi and interpreted its beauty.

The catalogue for The 3rd Nanjing Triennial (themed as Reflective Asia) is a project of word-formation, which is an extension of the exhibition's overall image. For headings and titles throughout the book, the studio has innovated new word-forms totaling several hundred characters, to give an effect which will correspond with the overall exhibition. White is the main color for the book. Moreover, readers will page through the book from right to left in Asian fashion, which reverses the normal left-to-right order of reading.

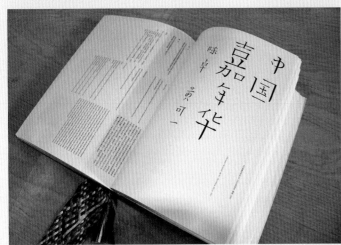

Bâtons Chiffres et Lettres is an essay about words, letters, and numbers by Raymond Queneau who is widely known for his unique experimental writing style in his prominent works. Kanji with its origin in pictograph has symbolic meaning from the beginning. To match the author's witty and humorous writing style, the designer decided to detach the symbols from their original meanings, and considered them simply as shapes, and then combined the pictorial images of the meaning to each letter, just like "Emoji".

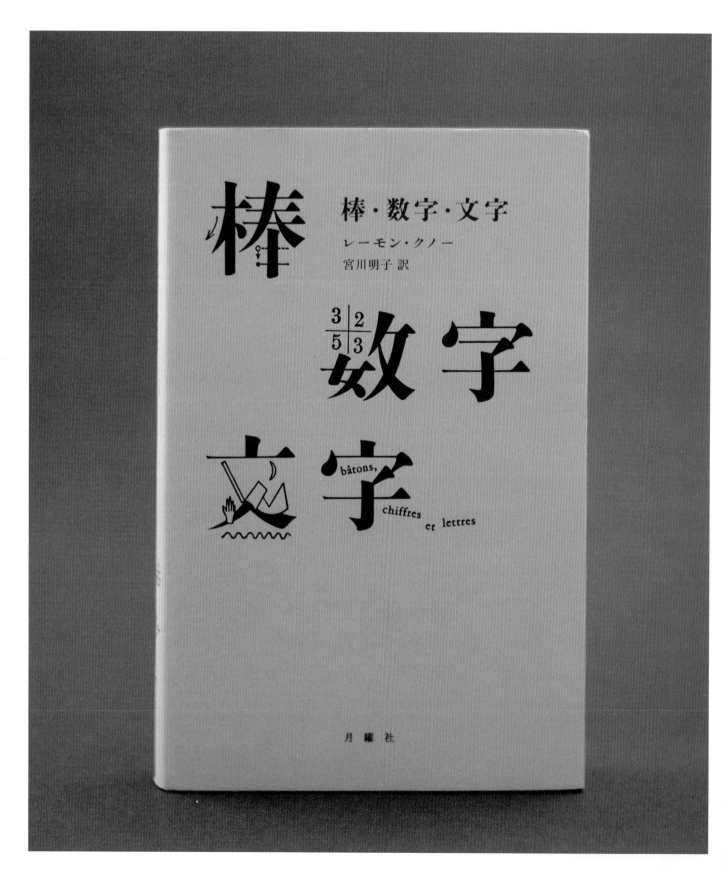

Kako's Tales of the Photography and Life of Shoji Ueda

Design: Ikuya Shigezane
Client: Heibonsha

This is an essay about Japanese Avant-garde staging photographer Shoji Ueda, narrated by his daughter Kako-chan, setting the rural landscapes of Japan in the 1960s' as the background, and revealed Ueda's working on his photography behind the scenes and his unique photographic style.

Instead of digital fonts, hand-written letters are used on the cover which add a warm and nostalgic touch to the book to represent the candid figure of Ueda, a renowned photographer, and a father.

Race Against The Machine

Design: *Asami Sato*
Design Agency: *Cozfish*
Client: *Nikkei Business Publications*

The book *Race Against The Machine* talks about how technology is accelerating productivity and irreversibly transforming employment and economy. Influenced by the theme of Proletarian protests, this book's printing, paper and monograms are meant to portray an image of labour. The design evoked an image of Proletariat with its use of modern typography, showing that co-existence and partnership between people and technology can bring positive outcomes.

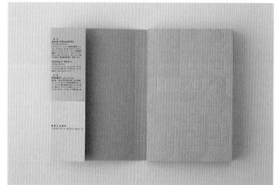

The author Taro Igarashi was invited to write a book explaining the reasons why Japanese architects are globally recognized and popular. The designer expressed his own impression of Japanese architecture—Minimalism, Zen, and sensitivity through types on the book jacket.

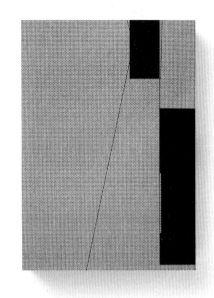

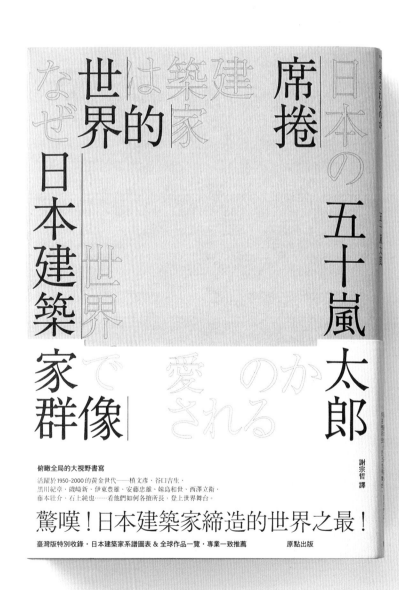

俯瞰全局的大視野書寫

活躍於1950-2000的黃金世代——槙文彥、谷口吉生、
黑川紀章、磯崎新、伊東豊雄、安藤忠雄、妹島和世、西澤立衛、
藤本壯介、石上純也……看他們如何各擅所長，登上世界舞台。

驚嘆！日本建築家締造的世界之最！

臺灣版特別收錄・日本建築家系譜圖表＆全球作品一覽・專業一致推薦　　　　　原點出版

Nobushi, Nishi E

Design: *Yiche Feng*
Client: *Rye Field Publications*

The book *Nobushi, Nishi E* (Samurai, Go West) is about short stories happened in a long walk from Tokyo to Osaka. To correspond to the idea, the map is printed in dark yellow colour as a background. The wild typography of the title was handwritten using the Chinese calligraphy brush, echoing the samurai spirit. This inner cover is printed as duo-tone instead of CMYK inks, and all the Japanese Kanji on it are the names of the places mentioned in the book.

野武士，一路向西

《從東京散步到大阪，兩年間的即興遠征》

每個假日的出征，都是為了讓回家時的俺更加勇敢。
背起烏克麗麗，俺就是江戶時代的野武士，從東京沿著舊東海道出發，
沒有網路，沒有地圖，沒有行程表，不認識路也沒關係，
一路向西走向大阪！

久住昌之
游韻馨/譯

之/著
/譯

麥田

For the cover design of this famous Chinese poems collection, the designer took six elements: wind, star, rain, flower, snow and water, and turned them into six graphic symbols. To match with the graphical Chinese characters "四" (four), "月" (month), and "天" (day), together meaning the April, the designer arranged these different elements in a strictly regulated layout. The designer presented the emotional poetic imaginations of April in a rational architectural analysis.

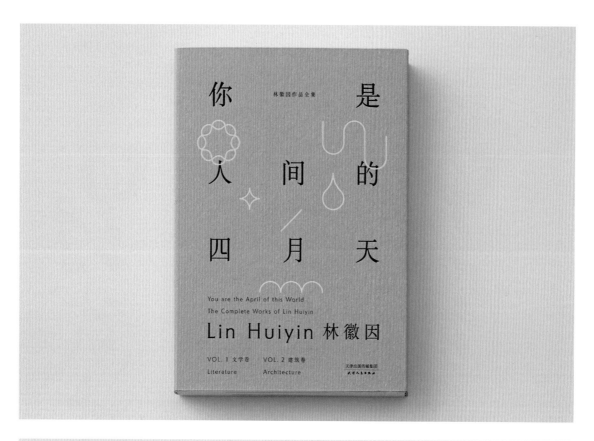

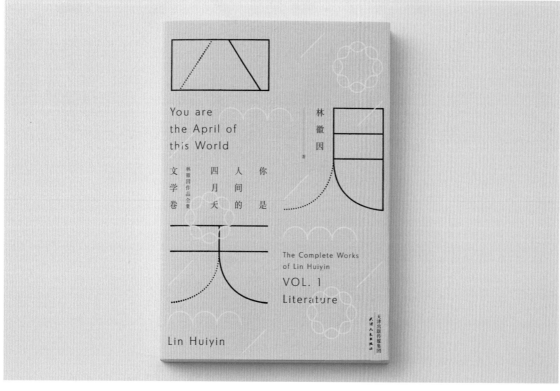

A Chinese Font Walk

Design: **Wang Zhi-Hong**
Design Agency: **Wang Zhi-Hong Studio**
Client: **Faces Publishing**

Graphic designers passionate about the Chinese language often enjoy deconstructing characters to achieve a better understanding of the constituent parts of individual characters. The act of walking usually implies distance and destinations. On the book cover, the designer took apart the strokes of the characters in the title "字型散步" (*A Chinese Font Walk*), aiming to inspire people with aesthetic perception of characters.

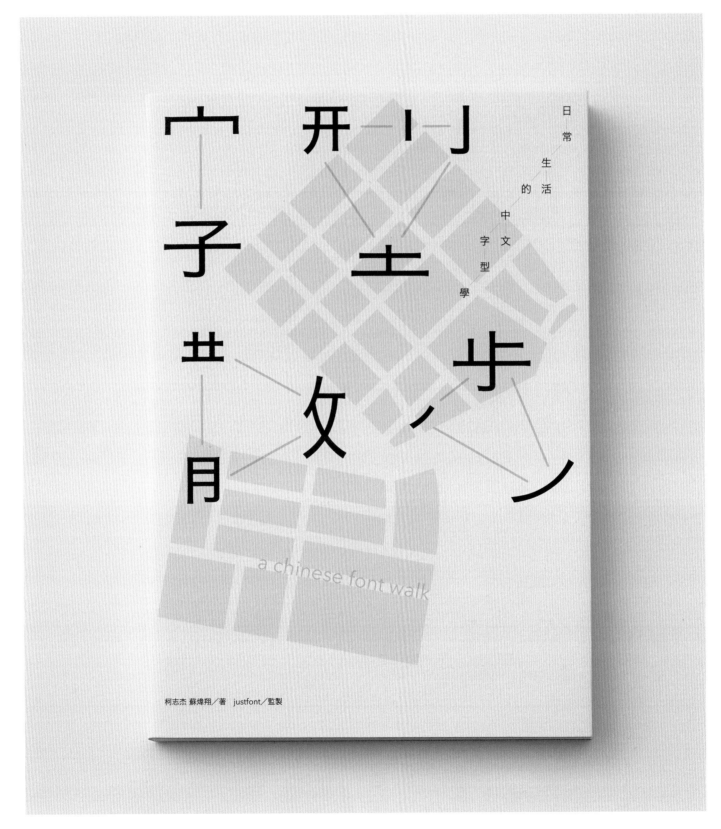

Memories of Back

Design: *Wang Zhi-Hong*
Design Agency: *Wang Zhi-Hong Studio*
Client: *Faces Publishing*

After reaching adulthood, how do people come to re-understand the structure of those characters with which they have been familiar long ago? The designer tried to recall how characters looked to him as a child and searched for clues in memories of feelings, but the proportions were not very accurate and several had too many lines. To take a different approach, he decided to present these reflex actions that perhaps once existed in his memory in the design. Nagashima Yurie wrote this book to give form to memories on the origins of things and images that have never been photographed or filmed, yet remain forever in our heads. As such, the cover was designed to encourage one to explore his memories.

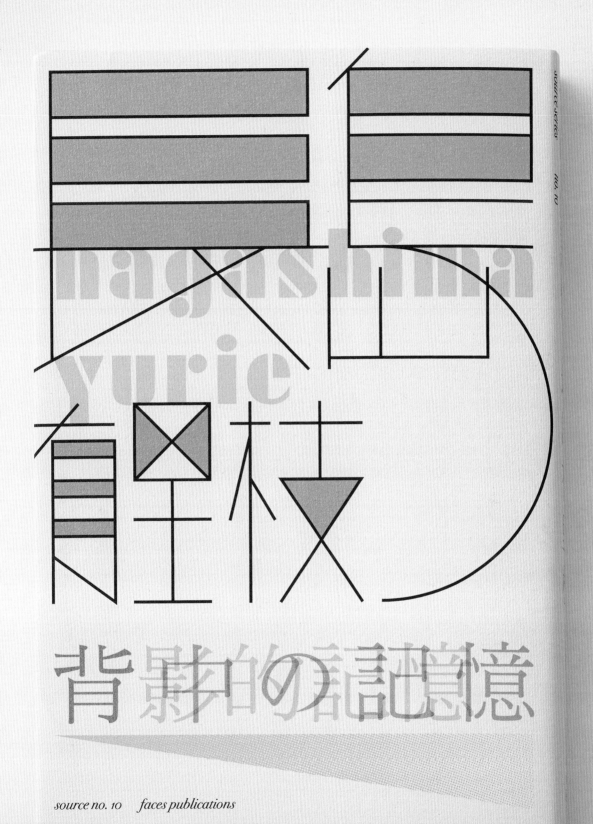

source magazine no. 10

長島有里枝

nagashima
yurie

背影的の記憶

source no. 10   faces publications

Nostalgic Printed Matter Museum of The Family

Design: *Yoshimaru Takahashi*
Design Agency: *Kokokumaru Inc*
Client: *Mitsumurasuikosyoin*

This is the cover design for the book *Nostalgic Printed Matter Museum of The Family*, a collection of Japanese package and label design over the past 50 to 100 years. The book is divided into different parts according to different family users. The logotype of the book title and family members are all original works of the designer.

レトロな
印刷物
ご家族の
博物館

お父様
お母様
お嬢様
お坊ちゃん
お嬢ちゃん

Retrospective Medicine

Design: **Yoshimaru Takahashi**
Design Agency: **Kokokumaru Inc**
Client: **Mitsumurasuikosyoin**

This book is a collection of Japanese drug packages and advertisements over the past 200 years. The titles of the book and each chapter are all shown with logotype specially made by the designer. The names of the medicine are constituted by soft curves to give a nostalgic feeling.

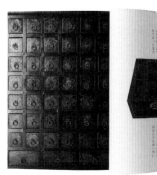

Hyakki Yako In & Yo

Design: *Yiche Feng*
Client: *Apex Press*

Hyakki Yako In & Yo is a combination of two books about the tales of terrifying yet comical demons set in postwar Japan. Considering the dark and mysterious tales, the cover carries the feature of Japanese books in the old times, reflecting the characteristics of that age. The logotype used in the title with modern retouching is based on the calligraphies for prints in postwar Japan. The In & Yo (陰陽) elements on the cover directly show the temperature difference, and the use of light orange and dark blue visualizes the impression of In & Yo.

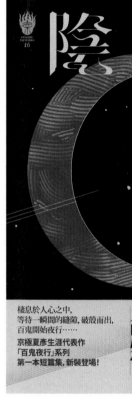

棲息於人心之中，
等待一瞬間的縫隙，破殼而出，
百鬼開始夜行⋯⋯
京極夏彥生涯代表作
「百鬼夜行」系列
第一本短篇集，新裝登場！

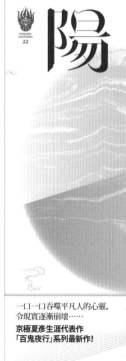

一口一口吞噬平凡人的心靈，
令現實逐漸崩壞⋯⋯
京極夏彥生涯代表作
「百鬼夜行」系列最新作！

This book introduces the modern decadent
works in Japan. To show the theme of
Tanbi, the design used a lot of gold leaves on
a black lace. The Kanji "幻想耽美" in the
title were integrated with Gothic patterns.

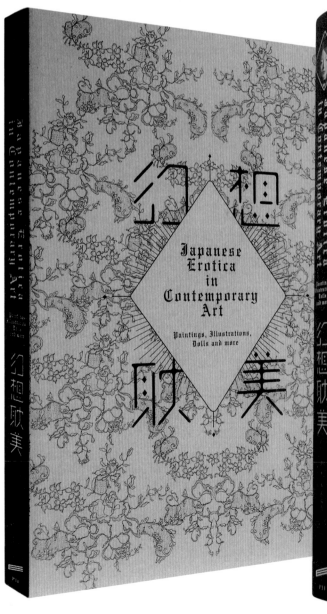

The Water Knife

Design: *Peng Hsing Kai*
Design Agency: **Empty Quarter Workshop**

The Water Knife is a science fiction novel that narrates the story about humans launching wars for water resource in the future. Its Chinese title "焚城记" literally means the tale of a burning city. The designer manifests the idea of burning with an image. In the design of the logotype, the piled-up characters represent the dimension of time and echo with the cylindrical structure of "城" (city). Readers may find the transition between reading the title and viewing the design interesting.

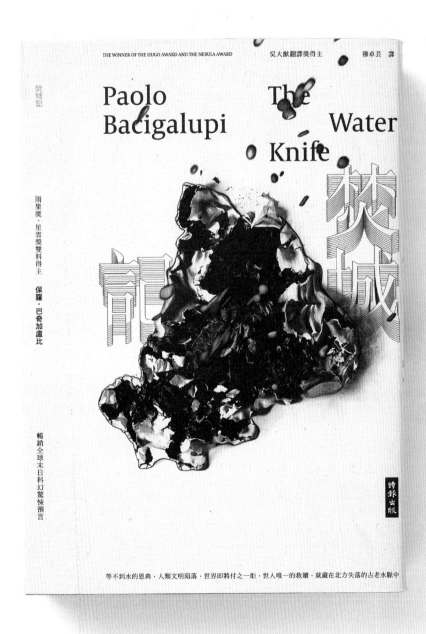

Cubed: a Secret History of the Workplace, as its name suggests, chronicles the evolution of the office. This book looks at one of its traditional Chinese versions, entitled "隔間" (meaning separated cubed spaces). The title "隔間" is interpreted in a visual way on the cover. The designer played with the two traditional Chinese characters: their strokes are printed on a semi-transparent book jacket, but in opposite directions and separated by a fold. When the jacket is folded along the folding line, the strokes appear in the right place and the complete characters "隔間" appear. The semi-transparent book jacket is a reflection of the word "secret" in the subtitle.

Stories of the Supernatural

Design: *Wang Zhi-Hong*
Design Agency: *Wang Zhi-Hong Studio*
Client: *Apex Press*

The cover design was for a collection of ghost stories and it was the first publication in the brand new "Kwai books" series by Kyogoku Natsuhiko. The designer believes that ghosts and monsters are imbued with a very primitive desire and he wanted to use the design of standard Chinese characters to convey a force that science cannot explain, thereby creating an atmosphere that is both modern and primitive. The geometric lines also convey a sense of primitivism. The modernism comes from the non-natural expressiveness of the lines as seen in squares and triangles, whereas the primitivism is found in the simplicity of shapes that is akin to hieroglyphs.

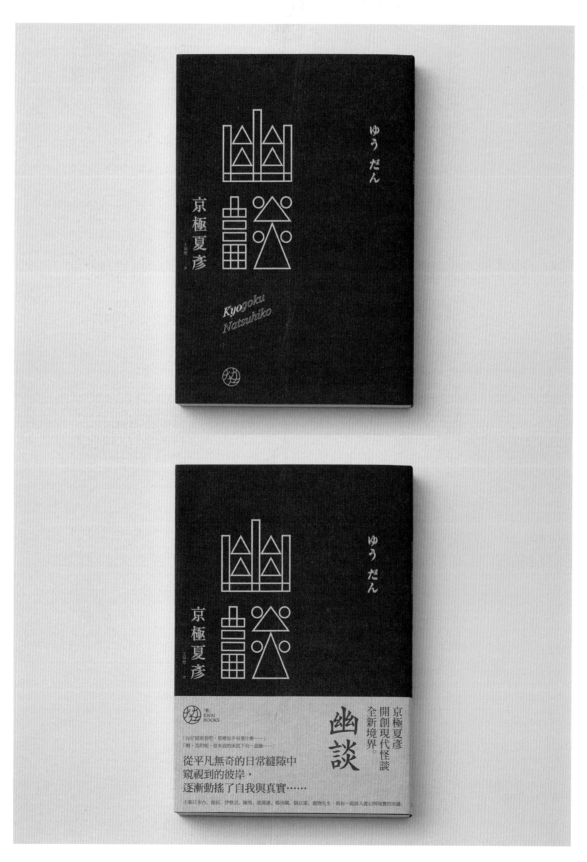

Mingteng Tea

Design: *Li Jianjie*
Design Agency: *Dowell Brand Design*

Mingteng tea encourages a healthy tea-drinking style. The boxes are made to mimic the shape of the waistline of cheongsam (a body-hugging one-piece Chinese dress for women), which is known for highlighting women's beautiful waistlines. The whole design, including its method of fastening, its typography, and the shape of the tea boxes, is an embodiment of Chinese cultural icons. The lines of the logotype is a reflection of the smooth texture of the tea.

THREE TYPES OF TEA A DAY

The stage play To Kill or To Be Killed (螳螂捕蟬), tells the story of two professional killers from South Vietnam and North Vietnam who were ordered to carry out a task in a hotel room. During the task, they had conflicts but also talked about the meaning of life. Based on the background of the story, the main visual of the design is infused with the style of the 1990s movie posters. A dynamic Chinese logotype was designed communicating the idea of "捕" (to capture) for the stage play.

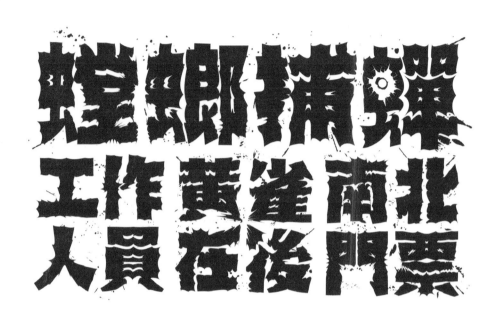

To Kill or to be Killed

誤會，矛盾，衝突
的事，都發生了⋯
兩個來自不同背景
因為執行任務被⋯
標出現期間，二人
毆鬥。在過程中⋯

導演的話

劇場是通向真理的⋯
演戲或看戲，都⋯
滿足對未知的好奇⋯
對生存的意義的好⋯
雖不是娛樂，但⋯
人間最高雅的享受⋯

潘惠森｜編劇

香港演藝學院戲劇⋯
加入香港演藝學⋯
於香港新域劇團⋯

話劇團於八十年⋯
創作不輟，在劇⋯
探索，形成了獨⋯
項。作為劇本創⋯
藝團合作，包括⋯
年輪》(1996)，新⋯
(2000)，劇場組合⋯

煙中的情感

所有不應該發生

現。

（北越和南越）

間裡，在守候目

翻翻，甚至互相

述自己對生命價

娛樂；而是為了

的本質的好奇、

味、可思考，是

前，潘惠森受聘

93-2012）。他的

甫受注目；其後

形式上進行持續

，並獲得多個獎

本地及海外多個

闖進一棵橡樹的

演出《貓城記》

虎》(2005)，德

黃樹輝｜導演

《螳螂捕蟬》是第四十五個導演作品。

Nakagawa Masashichi Shoten

Logo design: *good design company*
Product design: *Nakagawa Masashichi Shoten*

Nakagawa Masashichi Shoten is an old brand founded in Nara, Japan. It has a history of over 300 years, famous for its exquisitely hand-made linen products. The designer used character "七" in the brand name as the main element in the design of logo and made it the shape of linen clothes, the characteristic of its products. It conveys a home-life sense and good mood to the customers.

PEKING PIE

Design: *Gu Peng*
Design Agency: *GUPENG DESIGN*
Client: *PEKING PIE*

PEKING PIE is a souvenir bearing the spirits of modern Beijing. "Window lattice" were elements used in the packaging design. The designers selected twelve traditional window types to represent twelve landmarks in Beijing. And the Chinese characters for PEKING PIE—"北平派" are composed of the geometric shapes that used in the window types as strokes.

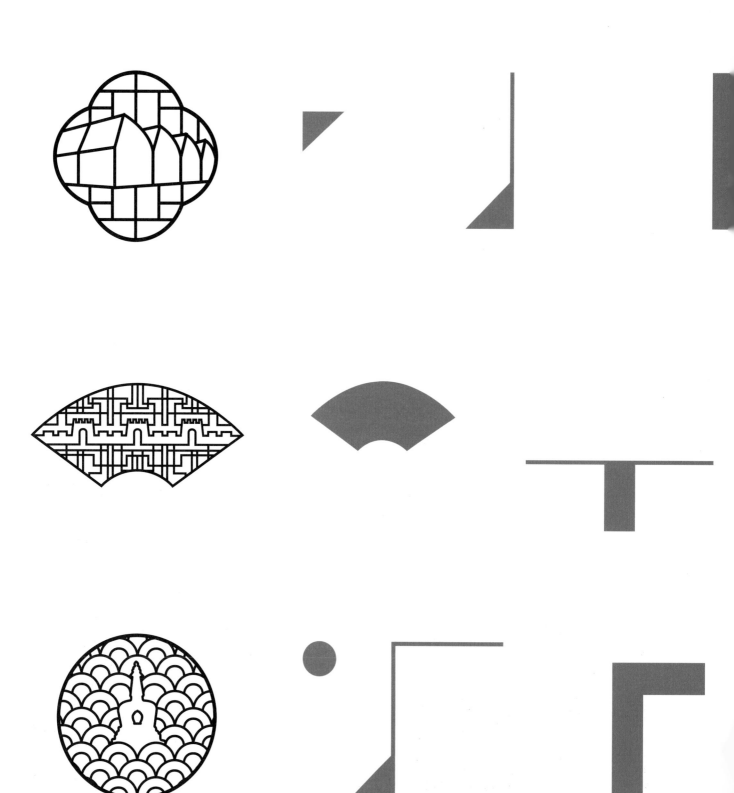

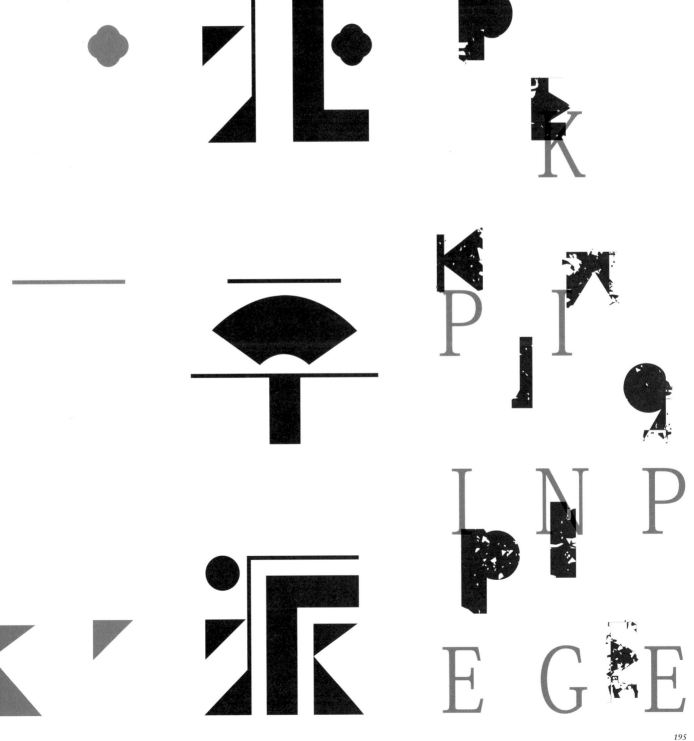

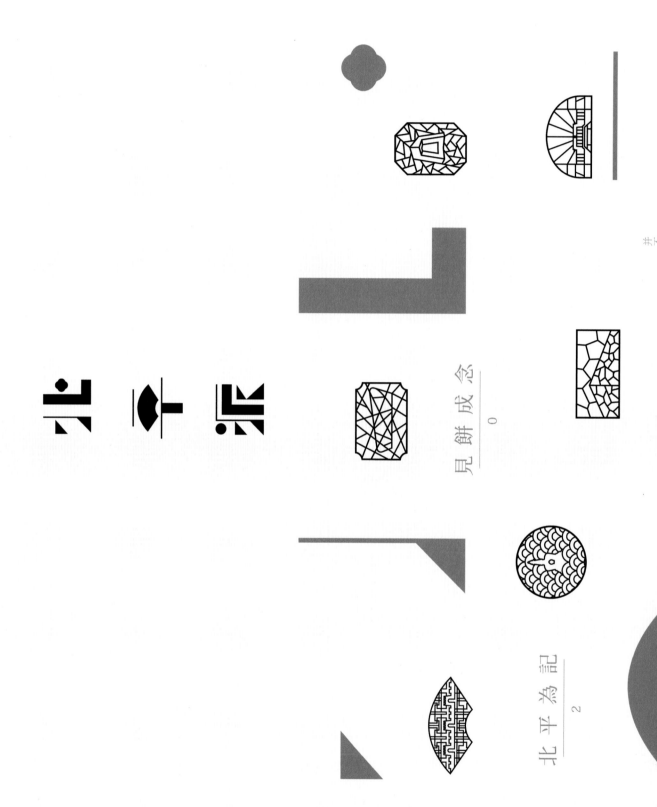

見餅成念

北平為記

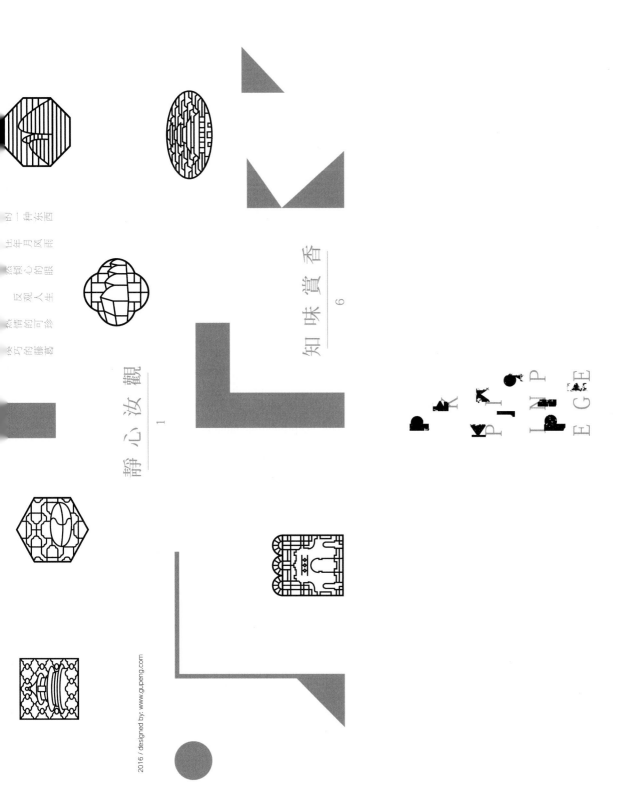

静心汝观
1

知味赏香
6

Kyoto Perpetual Diary is a collection of Japanese cuisine and Wagashi (Japanese confectionery) made for different seasons. With accordion binding, the book can be spread and wrapped with a red cord. The lovely finishing is meant to attract more female readers.

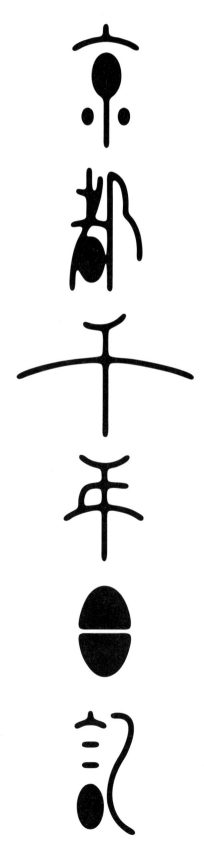

Time Travel Internet Cafes

Design: **Zeng Jiong**
Design Agency: **Chengdu Shi GuoShi Culture Communication Co.Ltd.**
Client: **Time-space Travel Internet Cafes**

To reflect the theme of time travel, the characters are built out of pixels based on the concept of four-dimensional space. Also the additional blocks of color suggest the uncertainties of time travel.

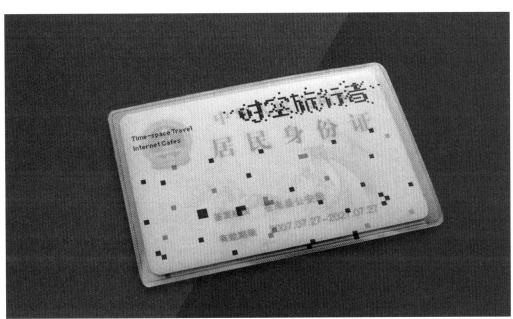

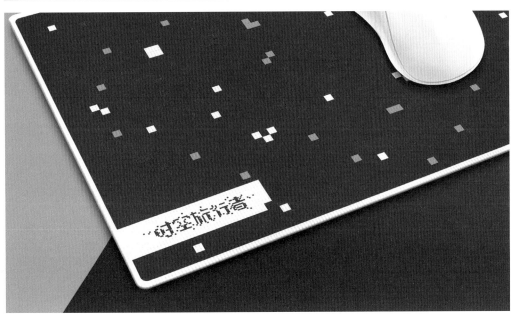

HAPPY GOAT (GOLD) YEAR

Design: *Arron Chang*
Design Agency: *EARLYBIRDS DESIGN*

The designers combined the shapes of Chinese character "羊" (goat) and "年" (year), and used color gold (as "goat" and "gold" sound similar in English), integrating these elements to a special literary image. Together with the pattern from the decomposition and arrangement of the strokes of Chinese characters, the designers completed a series of theme product packages to present to their clients.

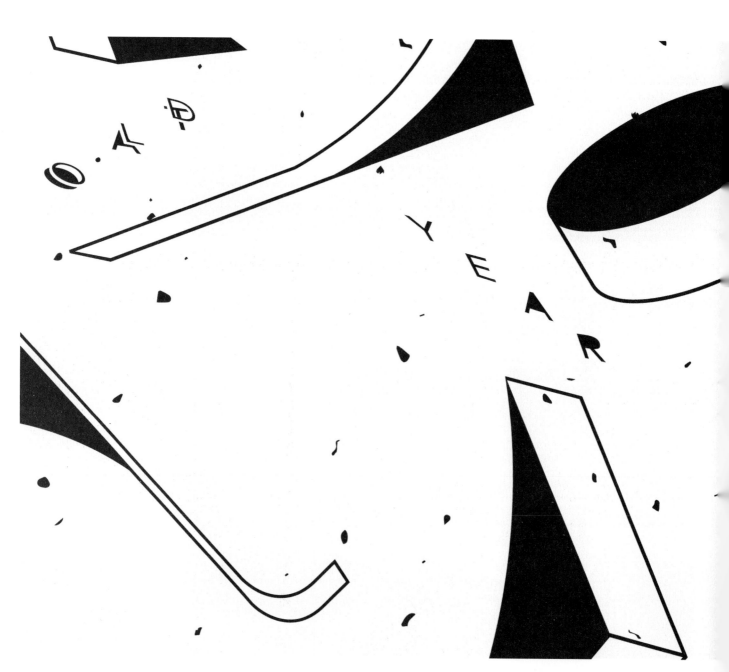

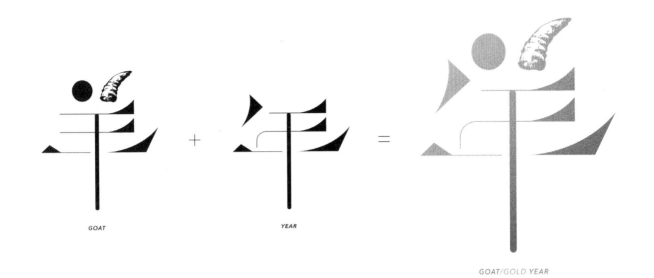

GOAT + YEAR = GOAT/GOLD YEAR

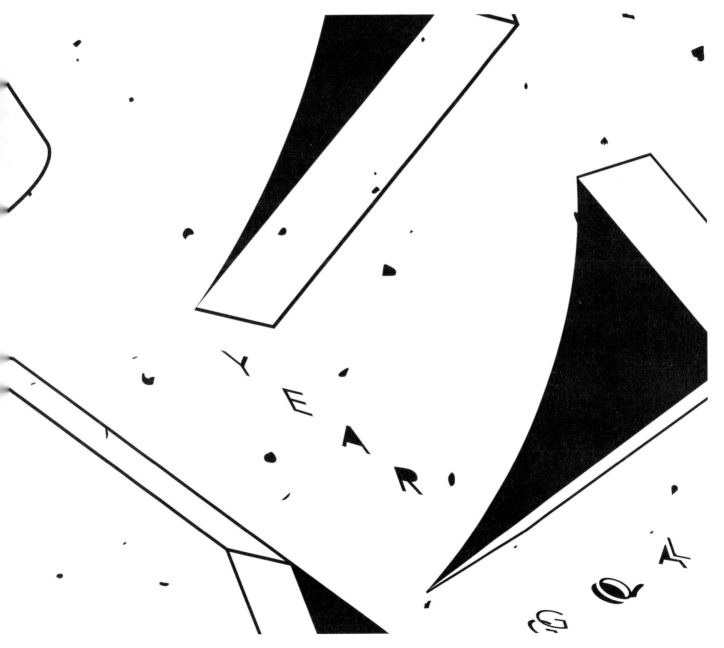

Tai Hang Fire Dragon

Design: Lai Man Ting Edmond
Design Agency: Much Creative Communication Limited

When the people of Tai Hang Village miraculously contained a plague with a fire dragon dance in the 19th century, they inadvertently launched a tradition that has since become part of China's official intangible cultural heritage. By means of the collage technique, the studio combined the Chinese lucky flags and Chinese calligraphy to constitute Chinese characters "舞" "火" and "龙" as the poster images. The bright lines and patterns on the dark background were to represent the burned incense to create a mysterious dancing backdrop.

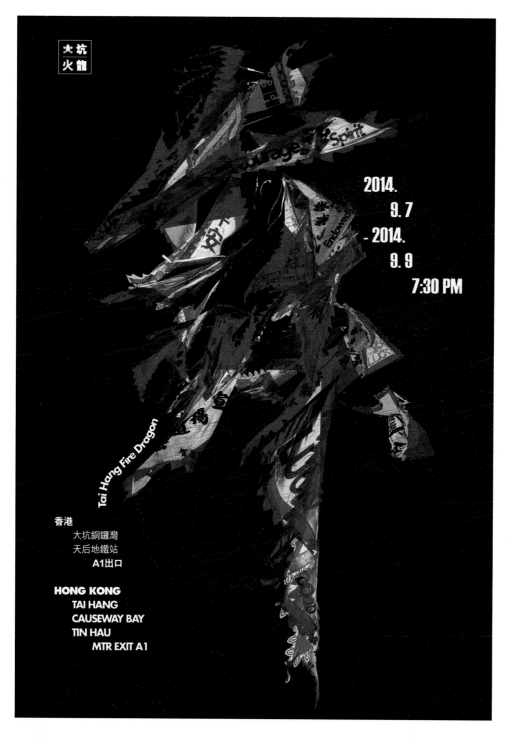

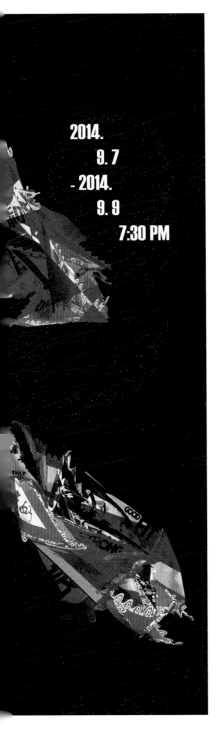

2014.
　　9.7
- 2014.
　　9.9
　　　7:30 PM

Tai Hang Fire Dragon

2014.
　　9.7
- 2014.
　　9.9
　　　7:30 PM

香港
　大坑銅鑼灣
　天后地鐵站
　A1出口

HONG KONG
　TAI HANG
　CAUSEWAY BAY
　TIN HAU
　　MTR EXIT A1

Panorama of Inner Journey

Design: *Ting-An Ho*
Client: **National Taiwan Museum of Fine Arts**

This visual identity was designed for the theatre project "Panorama of Inner Journey", themed "水生相" (The Water Ripples of Mind). To make the visual look more Oriental and Zen, the designer extended the strokes of logotype and transformed the text into graphics that flows like a quiet water drop. Through different ways that water flows, the logotype imitates the walking pattern of viewers and grows into a massive and evolving maze of identity.

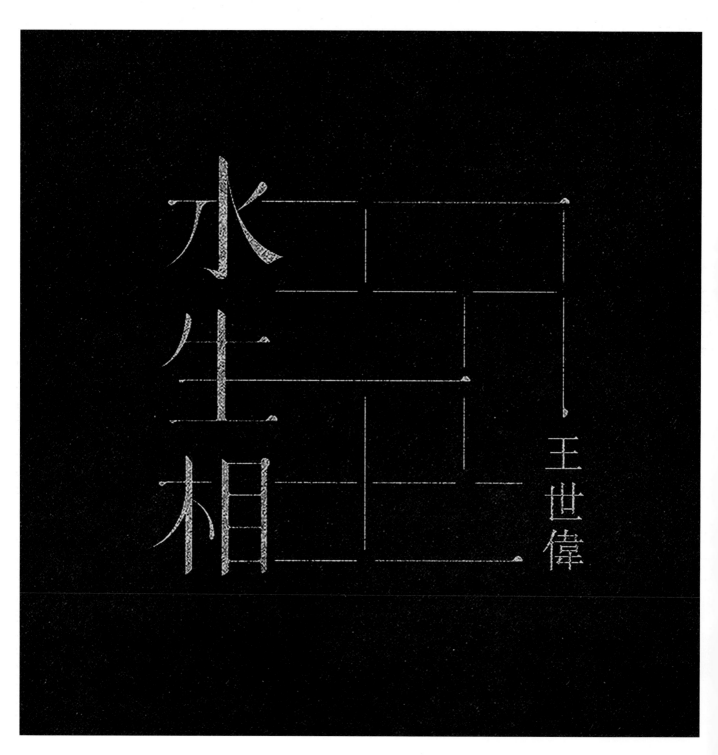

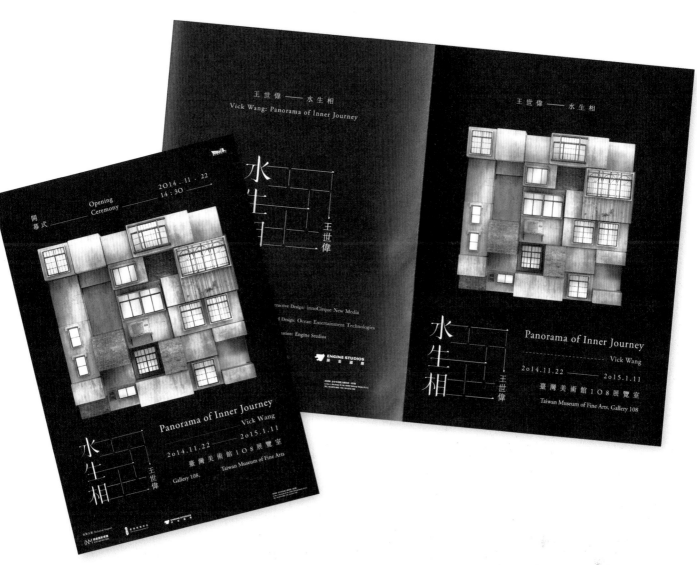

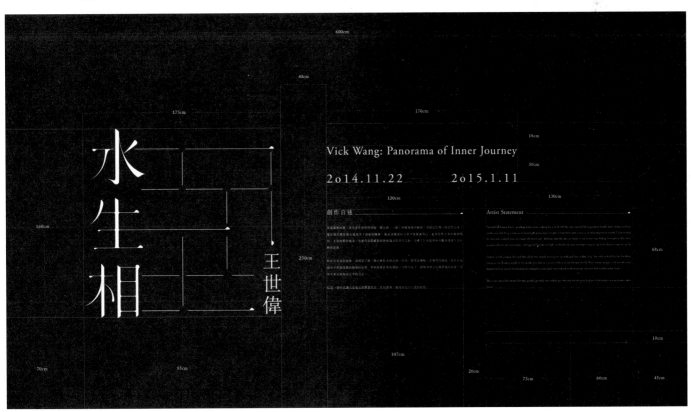

The logo is a combination of the calligraphy art dated
back to the early founding period of the Yungang
Grottoes and the special features of the grottoes itself.
Even the ending tips of the stroke in the logo is formulated
by the graphics on the grottoes. Traditional heritage has
always been the source of inspiration to the designer.

北魏文化節
THE NORTHERN WEI DYNASTY
CULTURE FESTIVAL

漫步云冈 梦回北魏
STROLL THROUGH
YUNGANG

DREAM OF THE
NORTHERN WEI
DYNASTY

YUNGANG
GROTTOES

北魏文化節
THE NORTHERN WEI DYNASTY
CULTURE FESTIVAL

漫步云冈 梦回北魏
STROLL THROUGH
YUNGANG

DREAM OF THE
NORTHERN WEI
DYNASTY

YUNGANG
GROTTOES

北魏文化節
THE NORTHERN WEI DYNASTY
CULTURE FESTIVAL

漫步云冈 梦回北魏
STROLL THROUGH
YUNGANG

DREAM OF THE
NORTHERN WEI
DYNASTY

YUNGANG
GROTTOES

北魏文化節
THE NORTHERN WEI DYNASTY
CULTURE FESTIVAL

漫步云冈 梦回北魏
STROLL THROUGH
YUNGANG

DREAM OF THE
NORTHERN WEI
DYNASTY

YUNGANG
GROTTOES

Kong Branding

Design: *Kevin He*
Client: *Kong Studio*

The logo mark is based on the Chinese character "空" (pronounced kong, meaning emptiness). Kong represents founder Kevin He's creative philosophy about spatial treatment—"a good graphic design is not how one controls the design elements but how one controls the empty space". The Chinese character "空" pervades the identity in various forms, ranging from leitmotif to empty space. It is a monogram derived from Kevin He's initial, K.H. Kevin also designed a custom font as part of the project based on both Chinese and English variants.

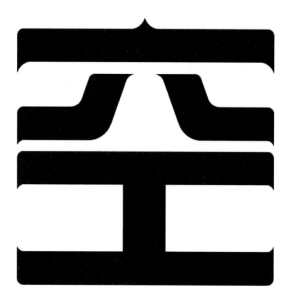

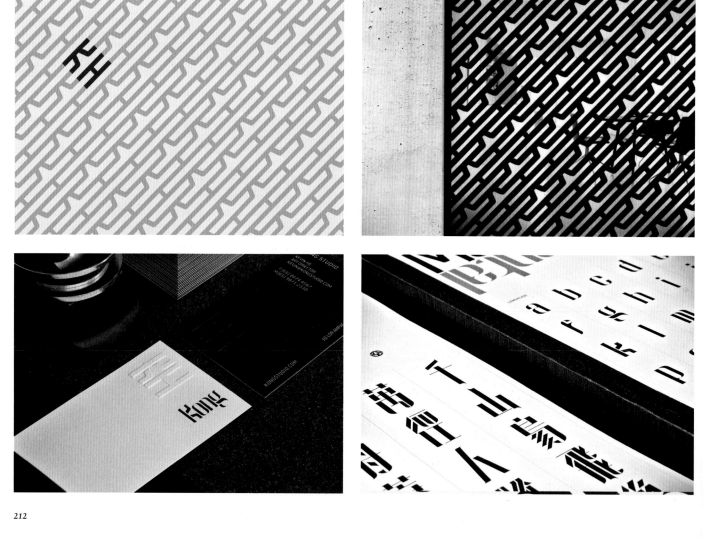

江雪

千山鳥飛絕

萬徑人蹤滅

孤舟蓑笠翁

獨釣寒江雪

横

竖

点

撇

横折

捺

提

竖折/竖弯

竖钩

横钩

Simplified

竖弯钩

横折弯

横撇弯钩

横折提

横折钩

横撇

竖提/斜钩

弯钩/竖钩

横折弯钩/横斜钩

竖折折钩

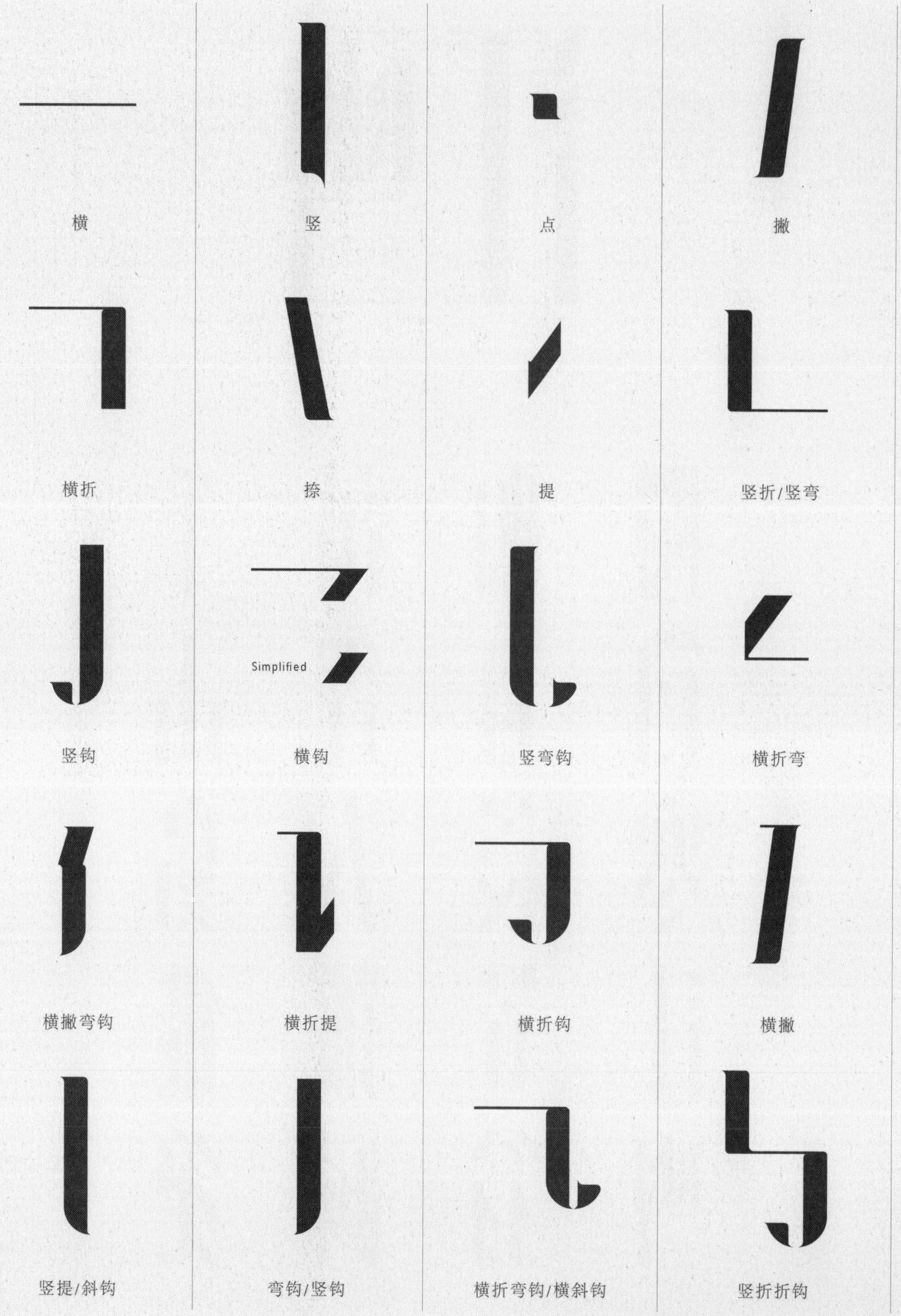

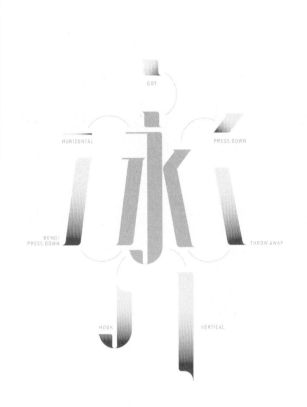

※ A CHINESE CHARACTER WITH A HIGH VARIETY OF STROKES.

DOT

HORIZONTAL

PRESS DOWN

BEND/
PRESS DOWN

THROW AWAY

HOOK

VERTICAL

Strokes of Chinese Characters

Design: **Lai Man Ting Edmond**
Design Agency: **Much Creative Communication Limited**

The Chinese characters on the poster were developed and transformed from the type fonts of the English word "much" on the logo, describing the philosophy, corporate image and culture of "Much Creative Communication Limited". By combining the English and Chinese characters, the creative group presented a perfect combination of Chinese calligraphy and Western writings.

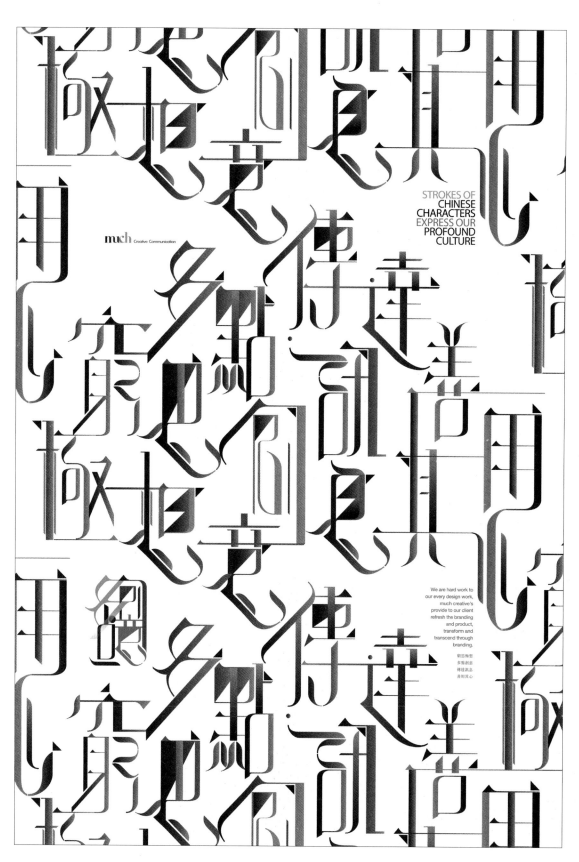

The Heart Sutra

Design: *Lai Man Ting Edmond*
Design Agency: *Much Creative Communication Limited*

Heart Sultra is known as a Buddhist classics to many people. The designer constructed the skeleton and strokes of the characters with Chinese modern typeface design approach and its design concept. And geometric and calligraphic elements are used in some finishing decoration. The whole arrangement of the fonts on the poster is by means of the grid system.

With a thoughtful approach, the designer used three paper cut patterns with auspicious Chinese idioms— "喜迎門楣" (the joyfulness of having a baby), "壽比南山" (best wishes for longevity) and "生龍活虎" (describing a person full of vim and vigor) as the main visual concept to match the meaning of a gift.Each box bears one of these three idioms to wish everyone health and happiness.

Who Cares—
Macau Social Issues
Art Exhibition

Design: Au Chon Hin, Lao Chon Hong
Design Agency: untitled lab
Client: OX warehouse

Who Cares—Macau Social Issues Art Exhibition offered local artists a platform to present their views on social issues through various forms of artworks. The patterns in the posters were created to mimic the image of a loudspeaker, highlighting the theme of this event to call on people to pay attention to the society. For consistency, the characters, numerals, and alphabets were constructed with the same colors and shapes in an irregular and creative way.

WHO CARES 關事 我 2015

MACAU SOCIAL ISSUES
ART EXHIBITION

策展人 CURATOR
郭恬熙 ALICE KOK

參展藝術家 ARTISTS

蔣靜華 CHEONG CHENG WA
何家永 CHRIS HO
尹保倫 VAN POU LON
阿聖奴 AQUINO DA SILVA
何志峰 HO CHI FONG
蔡國傑 CAI GUO JIE
何家政 HO KA CHENG
林鍵均 LAM KIN KUAN
夏天翔 HA TIN CHEONG
歐俊軒 AU CHON HIN
張智斌 CHEONG CHI PAN
劉俊康 LAO CHON HONG
梁祖賢 LEONG CHOU IN
歐陽永鋒 AO IEONG WENG FONG
霍凱盛 ERIC FOK
謝玉玲 CHE IOK LENG
何栢瀚 HO PAK HON
思崎井 CK CHEANG
梁加文 SIMON LEUNG
陸竹 PAL LOK

30/05

28/07

免費入場
FREE ADMISSION

澳門社會議題
藝術作品展

牛房倉庫 OX
Warehouse
Armazem
de Boi

IDEAL CITY—
TED×Kowloon
Salon 2013 August

Design: *Benny Leung*
Design Agency: *STUDIO-M*
Client: *TEDxKowloo*

This visual graphics project is a collaboration with TEDxKowloon
creative team for the Salon 2013 August themed IDEAL CITY.
Ideal and reality are more complementary than similar. The designer
explained this philosophy by the combination of two Chinese terms
with similar pronunciation in Cantonese "lei soeng/nei soeng"—
"理想" (ideal) and "你想" (you think). And a series of icons were
created to inspire the audiences' imagination of an ideal city.

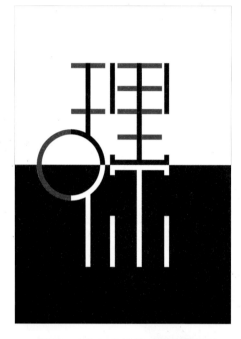

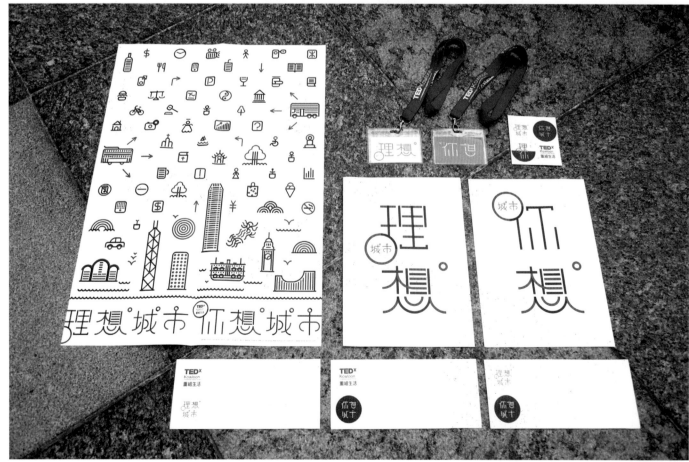

Located in IFC, a symbol of modern Hong Kong, Cuisine Cuisine is a contemporary Chinese restaurant which revolutionizes traditional Chinese cooking. The restaurant's chef is known to be a master of all the 36 Cooking Methods in Chinese cooking. The key branding element—the 36 Cooking Methods beautifully presented in time-honored Chinese calligraphy that tantalizes diners with every brush stroke—says it all. The brand collaterals, feature symbols of Cantonese cuisine including chopsticks, bowl of rice and teapot, marry traditional Chinese ink painting and contemporary hues of orange and red against a pristine white backdrop. Calligraphy, used to depict the tea gushing from the pot and the rice adorning the bowl, enhances Cuisine Cuisine's oriental image in the eyes of foodies. The result is a modern dining experience that borrows the best from traditional Chinese arts and crafts.

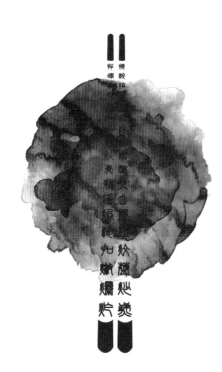

【撈】 Blend　　【醉】 Drunken　　【燒】 Red Cook　　【醃】 Salt　　【煙】 Smoke　　【烘】 Parch

【拌】 Dress　　【凍】 Chill　　【拼】 Pair　　【臘】 Cure　　【燻】 Smolder　　【烤】 Broil

【釀】 Stuff　　【煲】 Long-Simmer　　【滷】 Steep　　【煨】 Slow-cook　　【焗】 Casserole　　【炆】 Stew

【煮】 Boil　　【熬】 Decoct　　【醬】 Sauce　　【焗】 Roast　　【泡】 Gentle-fly　　【扣】 Double-steam

【滾】 Quick-boil　　【涮】 Scald　　【燴】 Simmer　　【蒸】 Steam　　【炒】 Sautéed　　【煎】 Pan-fry

【烚】 Poach　　【灼】 Blanch　　【扒】 Braise　　【燉】 Double-boil　　【爆】 Sear　　【炸】 Deep-fry

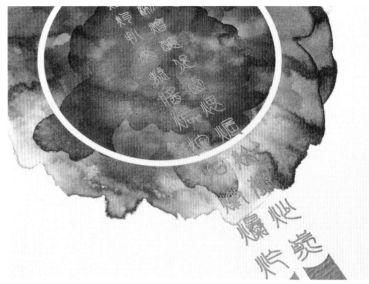

"Delicacies from the Mountains" is a brand that promotes healthy, ecological and pollution-free food from northeast China. The brand image reflects Chinese traditions and culture of maintaining healthiness and longevity by balancing "yin" and "yang". The undecorated logotype used in the logo helps to create an idyllic image of the harmonious relationship between human and nature.

Saudade Tea Package

Design: *Mariko Yamasaki, Mayuko Kato*
Creative/Art Director: *Yuji Tokuda*
Design Agency: *canaria Inc.*

The design is dedicated to a new organic Japanese tea brand, "Saudade". The brand sells selected green tea leaves to on-line shoppers all over the world. The new logo, the Chinese character "茶" (tea), was cleverly constructed with the letters in "saudade". The illustrations of tea-origins were created under the theme of "traveling with tea."

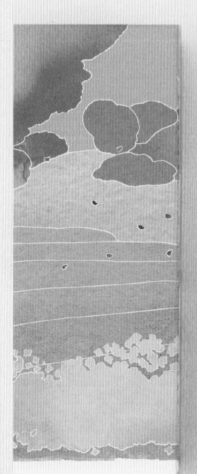

有機嬉野茶

温泉街にも近い自然に囲まれた佐賀嬉野の山間地で有機栽培された極上の茶葉は玉緑茶と言い、日本茶には珍しい独特の丸みを帯びています。嬉野産特有の甘み、艶やかな色味、とろけるような旨みの絶妙なバランスは癖になります。

Premium
Organic Green Tea

Ureshino

有機嬉野茶

Organic
Ureshino Tea

Made from the finest organic tea leaves cultivated in the mountainous hot spring area of Ureshino. The fascinating light color and perfect harmony of sweet and savory notes make it impossible to resist.

www.saudad

COLORFUL HOME's products feature a wide variety of styles and materials in all sorts of colours. After studying Chinese Pictograms, the group refined the Chinese character "色" (color) as its core graphic elements They also combined the charming and elegant temperament with Chinese folding fan to create an artistic oriental design concept.

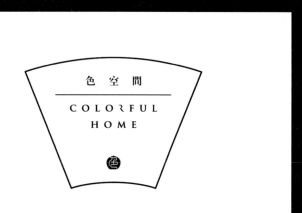

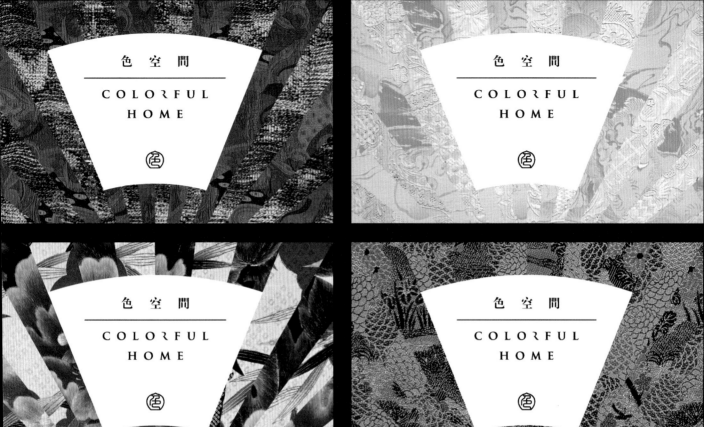

Nagoya Japanese Cuisine

Design: *Wen Li*
Design Agency: *One&One Design*

Nagoya Japanese Cuisine is a Japanese cuisine brand located in Pairs, France. The designer created the visual promotion system with the natural beauty of Oriental Zen all along. Known as washoku, Japanese cuisine highlights the natural and original taste of the ingredients, which reflects the Japanese spirit of respecting the nature. Therefore the slightly but deliberately clumsiness yielded in the visual system represents a typical spirit of "Zen".

www.nagoya.fr

0 Rue de Vaugirard
006 Paris
45 49 23 38

Rue Brey 75017 Paris
45 72 61

Bd du Montparnasse
015 Paris
45 72 61 88

Yen Yen is an experimental film about dreams and realities inspired by a dissociative symptom—"derealization". "Yen" is the pronunciation of two Chinese characters: "淹" (to be drowned) and "烟" (smoke). Corresponding to the meanings, the two Chinese characters are merged with horizontal and vertical wavy dotted lines to recreate the forms. The horizontal lines developed from the semantic indicator "氵" (meaning water) of "淹", while the vertical ones from the semantic indicator "火" (fire) of "烟".

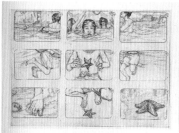

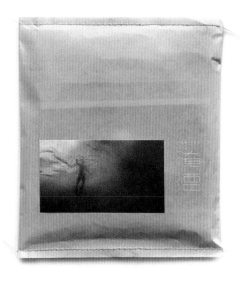

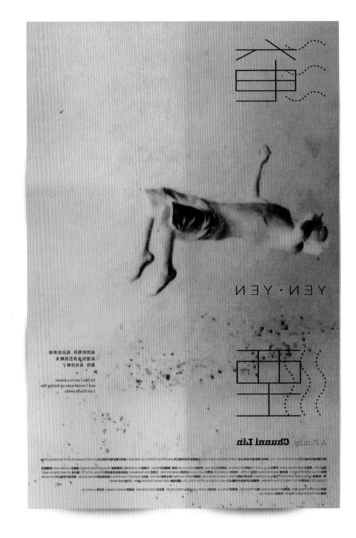

Tsai Chia-Hao Design
https://www.behance.net/tsaichiahao
P184-185

Tun Ho
behance.net/tunho
P134-135, P188-191

U

United Design Practice
uniteddesignpractice.com
P126-127

untitled lab
be.net/untitledlab
P220-221

V

Victor Branding Corp.
http://www.victad.com.tw
P218-219

W

Wang Zhi-Hong Studio
wangzhihong.com
P172, P173, P174-175, P186

Wen Li
www.behance.net/1and1design
P124-125, P158-159, P208-211, P234-235

WHITEr Design Studio
www.behance.net/rogerchuang
P236-237

Y

Yiche Feng
www.behance.net/yichefeng
P170-171, P180-181

Z

Zhan Wei
https://www.behance.net/zhanwei
P118-119

Photo Credit

A

Allen
https://flic.kr/p/5Dv33n
P20

Ah Wei (Lung Wei)
https://flic.kr/p/DvUmQU
P25

F

Francesco Crippa
https://flic.kr/p/dLGqFY
P21

G

GillyBerlin
https://flic.kr/p/21NGcw7
P25

K

Khitai
*https://zh.wikipedia.org/wiki/
File:Khitai5.jpg*
P21

M

Michael Coghlan
https://flic.kr/p/KjyoXc
P25

N

National Diet Library
Digital Collections
http://dl.ndl.go.jp/
P22

U

Uncle Hanzi
Hanziyuan.net
P28-95
(part of the glyphs in oracle bone
and bronze script in Part Two)

V

Valéran Sabourin
https://flic.kr/p/9cszTw
P25

W

Wikimedia Commons
https://commons.wikimedia.org/
P8-9,11-19,22-24

Wikipedia
*https://en.wikipedia.org/
wiki/Main_Page*
P8, 14

X

Xiquinhosilva
https://flic.kr/p/6f7Hnx
P21

Acknowledgements

We would like to thank all the designers
and contributors who have been involved
in the production of this book. Their
contributions have been indispensable in
its compilation. We would also like to
express our gratitude to all the producers
for their invaluable opinions and assi-
stance throug-hout this project. And to
the many others whose names are not
credited but have made specific input in
this book, we thank you for your con-
tinuous support.

Future Collaborations:
If you wish to participate in SendPoints'
future projects and publications, please
send your website or portfolio to

→ *editor01@sendpoints.cn*